Journaling
Fame

Date: 5/22/18

LAC BIO KUGEL
Kugel, Allison.
Journaling fame : a memoir
of life unhinged (and on the

Journaling Fame

A Memoir of a Life Unhinged
(and on the record)

Allison Kugel

Mill City Press, Inc.
2301 Lucien Way #415
Maitland, FL 32751
407·339·4217
www.millcitypublishing.com

ISBN-13: 978-1-63505-600-6

Printed in the United States of America

To Papa Morty, Nanny Thelma, Grandma Honore, my parents, brothers and my amazing son. You are my everything.

A special dedication to anyone living with anxiety or other emotional challenges, and the people who love them. We are in this together!

INTRODUCTION

The question I've gotten asked most regarding my journalism career had always been, "How did you get all these famous people to talk to you?" They're referring to my two hundred published interviews that were conducted by yours truly, over nearly a decade (2005-2014). I think they asked that because I'd managed to operate outside the traditional media fray. I never worked for an A-List publication, never went to school for journalism, and I spent the better part of my first eight years doing interview features for an online newswire that I helped to build and establish from the ground up, before resigning in the summer of 2012.

The reason, I would always tell them…trust. And I would also like to think, talent. But if I had to sum it up in one word, it would be trust. I maintained a stellar reputation of integrity and discretion. People trusted me to tell their stories and also to keep their secrets. I've leveraged my interviews into many headlines and notable media mentions over the years, created what the media would refer to as great "scoops," and I did it all without ever compromising my integrity or breaking my word.

When a public figure told me something was "off the record," that meant they were simply talking to *me*, person to person, in confidence. They expected that what they told me privately would be kept out of print and remain between us; same went for publicity types who represented these famous figures. I'd heard it all. Everything from divorce and custody issues to health issues, plastic surgery secrets and personal struggles. I know that many journalists, some very famous ones even, have gotten a bad rap over the years. It's no wonder; breaking promises, embellishing facts, using dirty reporting tactics to humiliate public figures, and going for the jugular in an interview have become commonplace. No finesse, no decorum. They go right for the money question and immediately put the celebrity on the defensive, and make them squirm. When all else fails, many simply make facts up. I always knew I was intelligent enough that when all the blood hungry sharks were circling the same potential headline of the moment, I could veer off in another direction and ask questions those other guys would never think to ask, thereby creating a headline in the media while keeping everyone's dignity, and the longevity of my reputation, intact.

Writing this book was especially challenging because many of you have probably picked it up hoping for some juicy tell-all tidbits, and yes, there is some of that sprinkled throughout these pages. While there are plenty of insights into my experiences with various celebrities (and behind-the-scenes goings on), I had to hold true to the word I gave to many of them when I specifically agreed to keep something private. So I worked on the 80/20 rule, leaving 80% of what I'd been told out of this book (anything I was expressly told was "off the record"). It's just how I'm built. This code of ethics was drummed into me by my father my whole life. If one of my two brothers or me told on each other, first we were lectured about being a tattle tale, or a rat. My father would say, "Nobody likes a rat. You don't do that to your siblings." Then he would deal with the issue at hand as a secondary matter.

However, my social life and my private life belong to me. If a relationship with an interview subject, or any public figure, bled into my private life, well that is part of my story which I feel I have a right to share. None of us lives our life in a vacuum. I'm not walking around in the twilight zone all by myself. I've interacted with and been affected by other people, as we all have. Those moments, like all of the moments of my life, have shaped me into who I am today. Those are fair game.

This book shares a portion of my life and intertwines much of my childhood and adolescence dealing with issues like anxiety and depression, as well as parts of my professional life as a journalist, with a few anecdotes of a personal nature sprinkled in. By no means is this my entire story, but handpicked moments that illustrate some significant emotional bridges and transitional times in my life which lent much of my evolution.

There are many stories, fun moments, awkward moments, observations and experiences that I *am* happily able to share and I hope you enjoy them. The chapters herein are an eclectic collection in both content and tone, as they reflect different sides to my character and the many different kinds of people that I chose to cover throughout my career as a journalist who interviewed newsmakers.

This book chronicles much of what was going on in my life, in my heart, and in my mind as I embarked on and eventually made a go of my crazy career. I'll weave my own roller coaster of a ride through the good times and the *not so* good times, throughout these celebrity interview passages, going back and forth between the two. I hope you can delve in and take this non-linear ride with me, both through the ups and the downs… through family moments, great laughs, bouts of emotional distress, losses, breakups, makeups, motherhood, personal reflection and triumph. These are (some of) my stories, and they just happen to include a job I had, Journaling Fame.

As I mused to musician Bret Michaels during my 2007 interview with him, "The one thing this job has taught me is that there is no magic carpet ride. We're all just people." To which he replied, "Bingo!" In fact, I felt a certain electricity during our hour long chat. I found Bret to be both boyish and manly in all the right ways. There was a connection made during the conversation. I was intrigued. At the end of our interview there was this brief hesitation after which he blurted out. "I'm going to be in Wantagh, Long Island, performing soon. I would like for you to come watch the show and come by afterwards to say hi. You can bring a friend… *or your husband??* Whoever you want."

I didn't have a husband at the time but I had just started dating my soon-to-be son's father, Patrick. I felt stuck between a rock and a hard place to be really honest with you. I liked Bret, but I felt bringing Patrick with me to the show would be the right thing to do as we had been dating for a few months by that point. The night of the show I strode up to the will call window at the Jones Beach Long Island amphitheater proud as a peacock, as I told the ticket vender that I had two tickets waiting for me, courtesy of Bret Michaels. After enjoying the concert from our second row center seats, Bret's longtime assistant, Janna, called me on my cell phone to find out where I was. They were expecting me to come onto the tour bus to say hello. She managed to work the question into the conversation of inquiring who I had brought with me. I answered truthfully; "I'm with my boyfriend." Janna seemed a little thrown by my answer. I picked up something in the tone of her voice. I didn't read into it further. Pat and I climbed up and into Bret's tour bus where he was winding down a pleasant conversation with some other well-wishers. He then turned to me and said, "There she is! We were wondering where you were." I stuck out my hand to shake Bret's and locked onto his big blue eyes.

With my new boyfriend right by my side, I have to tell the truth and admit I was taken with Bret's good looks. I thought, "Shoot. I kind of have a crush here. Awkward!" I broke the handshake and we all made conversation: me, Patrick and Bret. The conversation was lighthearted and mostly revolved around Bret's re-emergence into pop culture with his VH-1 show, *Rock of Love*, currently in its first season. I don't remember specifics other than that I sounded like a mumbling stuttering goofball because his baby blues had me transfixed. I'm typically into tall *dark* and handsome, so he wasn't even really my usual type. Sadly, I sounded nothing like the well-spoken, insightful journalist I had been during our interview days earlier. Towards the end, Bret offered, "Hey why don't you join us at a club tonight? We're going out after this."

I felt that the awkwardness of the situation would reach some kind of strange crescendo if Patrick and I went out with Bret. So I gracefully declined, saying it had been a fun night but we were going to head back home.

All in all, a weird set of thoughts rolled around in my head over the next few days. Did this mean I should break up with Patrick? How could I continue to date someone if I had eyes for someone else? Or was it just one of those fleeting little crushes that really meant nothing at all? I decided I would contact Janna and ask her to have Bret call me. If he returned my call I would put my other situation on hold. If he didn't, I would chalk it up to a great interview and fun meet and greet.

Although I did get a few funny and cute messages passed back and forth to me through Janna with Bret telling her to tell me that "Lovable Bad Boy Bret" *(a private joke)* said hello, no phone call materialized, and I let the whole thing drop. After all, he was even publicized through VH1 to have found "true love" at the culmination of the first season of *Rock of Love*. It was important for him and for VH1 to stay on message with that. A few days later I jokingly rationalized to a friend that Bret was a Type 1 Diabetic and Type 1 Diabetes runs in my family as well. "We could never have babies together anyway," I justified with a giggle and a shrug.

Shortly thereafter, my new tentative relationship with Patrick blossomed into a full committed relationship with the exchange of "I Love You's," and I didn't look back for six years from that point on. In fact, as my journalism career progressed with a parade of one famous heartthrob after another, Patrick and I had a running joke. Any time I would leave the house to go do an interview with a handsome movie star or musician, he would sheepishly and jokingly call out to me, "I *love* you… *Please come home*." And we'd both have a laugh. Once I was committed, I was committed and anyone else after that fell flat on me. No. There is no magic carpet ride. But at that time, after nursing a bruised heart from past relationships gone wrong and keeping Patrick at arms-length, I had finally let myself experience love again.

But I digress…

Even for those who actually walk red carpets, rest assured, there's no magic carpet ride. You really don't know what it's like to live in someone else's skin, what might have happened to them earlier that day, what goes on behind closed doors, or how someone feels inside even when they're smiling in flowing couture. The amazingly adorable sweet spirit, Kristin Chenoweth, drove that point home for me further when she told me, "There's definitely been times where I've had to put on a happy face even when I didn't feel like it, surely I have. There is a conception about me that I'm happy all the time; I wake up smiling, go to bed smiling, and life is great for me and I have no problems. That's obviously not true, because I'm human."

As much as I would have liked to recount all two hundred interviews in this book, there just wasn't enough space, so I chose certain moments and people who left an impression on me in one way or another. I also made a point to choose interviews that took place during some of the more emotionally charged or transitional times during certain periods of my life.

Journaling Fame

CHAPTER ONE

"I fear, fear itself. I'm a believer that if something is going to happen, it's gonna happen."-told to me by Mike Tyson

At 3 AM on a July morning in 2012 I lay aimless and helpless on an emergency room cot in my local hospital, unable to experience any emotion other than fear and the many physical sensations that racked my defeated body. The physical manifestations of extreme levels of anxiety that I was experiencing did not cease; my body showed me no mercy, perhaps because my racing mind did not extend that courtesy to my body.

I was wrapped in a backless hospital gown and a meagerly strewn blanket that had just been nuked in a microwave to keep me warm. I was uncontrollably shaking and shivering from the inside out. My body tremors felt as though they were growing worse with each passing minute as my entire body was wracked with quakes, shakes and frailty. I felt aches and pains and my eyes bulged with fright and confusion. "What is happening to me?" I thought.

"How did I get here? Am I going to die?" Perhaps my body would simply give out from the amount of stress I had unwittingly heaped on it in recent weeks.

As a chronic baseline anxiety sufferer my entire life, I was in the throes of the worst and most extended episode of acute anxiety I'd ever known. I was experiencing upwards of five or six full blown panic attacks per day, generalized fear, agoraphobia and unbearable physical sensations and symptoms. I feared I was dying, or worse, losing my mind completely and "going crazy," a common fear among those with anxiety and panic disorder.

All the while, I was maintaining a few lucid moments here and there to conduct my interviews and turn them in to my editor in time for publication. No one outside of my immediate family was the wiser.

In the hospital's ER…

A compassionate and physically disabled male nurse entered my room announcing that they would be "giving me something for the anxiety and panic" as he hoisted a bag of medicine onto the dolly that was connected to the open port in my right arm. The irony of his physical disability and limitations versus the emotionally driven sensations that *I* was experiencing was not lost on me.

I'd never taken any tranquilizers, benzodiazepines or other kinds, before in my life. In fact I steered clear of most medications and drugs altogether as they frightened me. With my existing fears of unknown medication and the persistent fear of experiencing an allergic or adverse reaction to a drug, I continued to press my nurse about the safety of the drug he was about to drip into my exhausted body. "What if this medication doesn't agree with me?" I protested. "What if I have an adverse reaction?" My nurse assured me, "I'm sure the medicine will agree with you just fine. Let us do the worrying." At that point I was in no position to argue. My entire body wracked with intense anxiety and panic, I had lost 10 lbs. bringing me to a pathetic size 0 from a once healthy size 4. I felt weak, defeated, scared and willing to try just about anything for some sweet relief. I blinked and nodded my head sheepishly. I watched as the Ativan made its way from the clear plastic bag, down the long thin tube, into the open port, and into my vein.

Within what felt like mere seconds, and for the first time in eight long and excruciating weeks, my body fell into a state of rest and release, albeit an artificial doped-up state. It was the kind of drugged haze where you don't even care if you truly exist or not. I had yet to master the natural state of release and compliance with the ebb and flow of the universe, and with God's plan for my life. I had yet to accept change as a natural part of life.

Just a few days prior to my hospitalization, I had interviewed Senator John McCain's outspoken daughter, Meghan McCain. Through my paralyzing anxiety I was able to gather myself when the phone rang and it was Meghan on the other line. She was promoting her book, *America, You Sexy Bitch: A Love Letter to Freedom*. Meghan co-wrote the book with actor and comedian, Michael Ian Black. As I sat in the kitchen of my home on Long Island, New York, waiting for the phone to ring, I turned to my mother who was tending to some dishes for me.

"I'm falling apart. How the hell am I supposed to ask Meghan McCain a bunch of in-depth political questions in the next two minutes? I can barely manage the most mundane tasks!" My mother replied, "You're a pro. You'll get through it. You always know how to pull it off." Of course she was right. I do have an uncanny ability to pull it together brilliantly when I need to, and interviewing public figures by that point came as naturally to me as breathing.

Between the time that Meghan's father had run for president in 2008 and this interview which took place four years later, I, myself, had transitioned from sworn Democrat to Middle of the Road leaning towards Republican.

Just before the phone rang, I noticed a technical failure with my digital recording device as I gave it my usual fail-safe last test before every interview. Before I could deal with the issue, Meghan was on the line, haggard and cranky from a long day of press interviews. I knew this was the last thing she wanted to deal with, but I said, "Meghan, I'm having a problem with my recorder and I want to make sure it's working properly. Would you mind saying 'testing 123, testing 123' into the phone before we get started?" In a flat monotone voice she robotically repeated, "testing 1-2-3… testing 1-2-3." By the grace of God, whatever the issue was had been fixed and we proceeded as I hyperventilated my way through the conversation.

For some reason my altered emotional state combined with her transparent media fatigue made me perhaps bolder than I would have normally been, or maybe that's just my delayed perspective on things. In any event, I hit the ground running. I asked Meghan why the Republican base finds her unappealing, and why they don't care for her identification with their party. I asked her about everything from firearms to Mormons. To Meghan's credit, her answers were full of candor, though her attitude kind of sucked. Yes, I said sucked. I know that description of Meghan McCain won't win me any literary awards, but graciousness was indeed lacking in her demeanor. Never one to cover up my thoughts, I came out and questioned whether I was making her angry. I could feel a pregnant pause of regret through the phone. Here's how that part of the conversation went down:

Allison Kugel: Being that you are a Republican who believes in gay marriage, the legalization and taxation of marijuana and women's sexual liberation and birth control, are you more to the left then you'd like to think?

Meghan McCain: No, I'm not. I told you I sway Libertarian, [socially]. I'm a Republican and I believe in our strong national defense. I am not a Democrat. I think angry Republicans like to label me that way, and I think some people don't understand what being a Republican means.

Allison Kugel: You sound angry.

Meghan McCain: I'm not angry, I just keep getting asked this all the time. I'm sorry I'm just very tired. I just, you know, I sway Libertarian.

Like many who are players within the Republican narrative, Meghan McCain had this to say to me about celebrities who voice their opinions about political and social issues:

Allison Kugel: I read your blog (*McCainBlogette.com*) very recently. You showed a clip of Sarah Jessica Parker, and I believe, Anna Wintour doing public service announcements for President Obama's re-election campaign. And in your book

you were calling out Al Gore and Leonardo DiCaprio, for being out of touch with the average American's financial ability to "go green." What is it about celebrities getting involved with political and social issues that riles you and turns you off?

Meghan McCain: In the book when we were talking about Al Gore and Leonardo DiCaprio we were discussing climate change. Why a lot of Republicans were turned off is because they don't want to be lectured to by Hollywood millionaires that take private jets to and from places, and are probably making a much larger carbon footprint than any average American. They seem very out of touch when they are preaching about it. I personally do believe in climate change, and I think we should start talking about it in a realistic and not so ominous way. I just think they don't realize how they've put the movement back in relation to talking to "real Americans," although I don't love the term "real Americans." You know, average Americans. The Sarah Jessica Parker ad, I just think it's disrespectful to call the President "my guy." I'm obviously not voting for President Obama and I couldn't vote for President Obama, but I just thought it was disrespectful to the Oval Office and to the President, himself. It's ironic because they put the ad out, themselves, and I just didn't like that.

Allison Kugel: Sarah Jessica Parker put her ad out independently?

Meghan McCain: No, I think it was a club that the Obama campaign created to promote the dinner she was having at her house; a fundraiser I believe.

So here's the thing… a lot of what Meghan said to me made sense, and I admired her intelligence and her perseverance to continue to be a relevant voice for the right, while maintaining some staunch beliefs that clearly sway liberal.

However, my opinion of her was that of someone whose intelligence is holier-than-thou and condescending rather than of wanting to impart information and share her views in a charitable and humble way. If I wanted clarification on her point-of-view or if I asked her a question that she deemed too pedestrian for her liking, I could basically feel an eye roll through the phone.

Now, to be fair and balanced in my opinion, I don't think Meghan wanted to discuss her personal feelings about the 2008 presidential election or about her take on fellow political celebrities' opinions of her or her family. She wanted to discuss issues, rather than anything that could be churned and burned into gossip fodder. I respected that for the most part. Here is what she had to say about her dad's loss of the 2008 presidential election from a daughter's perspective, as well as that long ago Meghan McCain/Bristol Palin feud:

Allison Kugel: Everybody had their opinion about who they thought should be president back in 2008, but no one but you and your siblings are the children of the losing opponent. Most people, obviously, have no idea what that feels like.

Meghan McCain: I was obviously sad when he lost, but I'm a big believer in things always happening as they should. I'm not really big on hanging on to the past or being angry about the past. I think that's kind of an unhealthy way to live.

Allison Kugel: Was the whole Bristol Palin/ Meghan McCain feud something that was hyped by the media?

Meghan McCain: I think anything anyone is going to say about her or me is just manifested by the media. Honestly, I never think about Bristol Palin unless I am being asked about her. We are just such different people and live such different lives, and I wish the Palins nothing but the best.

When I asked Meghan if she felt her father was robbed of his destiny to become president of the United States, she laughed at me; not *with* me and not at my question. She laughed *at* me. And, yes, I could tell the difference. I thought it was a fair enough question, but to her it was nonsensical and frivolous.

Allison Kugel: Do you think your father was robbed of his destiny to become President of the United States?

Meghan McCain: No, I don't. No. I think the definition of someone's destiny is that it happens exactly as it should. I think President Obama won in a fair fight. Would I have preferred my father winning? Of course! I don't know if my father thinks like that either.

I then moved on to more typical fare:

Allison Kugel: Have you ever thought about requesting an interview with President Obama to air your concerns about some of his policies and get direct feedback from him?

Meghan McCain: I don't think he would say yes, quite frankly . I don't think he would want that.

Allison Kugel: *(Laughs)* **Are you as much of a fan of Ronald Reagan as so many Republicans are?**

Megan McCain: Yeah, I think you get your Republican card taken away from you if you don't love Ronald Reagan . But I do genuinely have a great fondness for him as I think so many Republicans do.

Allison Kugel: What is it that makes Ronald Reagan the gold standard of the Republican Party?

Meghan McCain: He was the president during a real kind of renaissance time for Republicans, many of the things he stood for have become big platforms for Republicans ever since, and he really was a uniter. He was a bipartisan president and extremely inspirational.

Allison Kugel: Do you think we'll see somebody with that kind of bipartisan spirit again, anytime soon, in the oval office?

Meghan McCain: I hope so. I think Mitt Romney is trying to. Is it going to be quite like the golden era of the Reagans? I don't know. I don't think anyone can really predict that, but I certainly hope so.

As the conversation drifted into territory that was more to Meghan's liking I could feel her defenses drop a bit and her demeanor soften. She retained her "been there, done that" attitude, but I can only imagine how many journalist questions she had racked up from her days on the 2008 campaign trail to that day in the summer of 2012 when she and I spoke about her book. I got through the interview and managed to file the story on time.

As agoraphobia *(something that has haunted my mom on and off for decades)* strengthened its grip on me and even the simplest activities like taking a shower or walking to my mailbox filled me with fear and dread, I flashed back to an interview I had done with boxing legend, Mike Tyson, in April of 2012. Mike has had a tremendous amount of highs and just as many lows in his lifetime. But his demeanor with me was very fluid, like someone who has resigned themselves to the powers of the universe after decades of fruitless pushback against it… he is at peace with what is. I found it fascinating to ask someone who had been so feared in the boxing ring, what *he* was afraid of.

His answer?

"I fear, fear itself. I'm a believer that if something is going to happen, it's gonna happen. Hard times come upon everyone. I'm just happy the only person [sic] I have to worry about is God.

Other than that I don't fear anything. And I
respect everyone. From an omnipotent point of
view, I just [fear] God. I'm afraid of everybody, but
I'm not intimidated by anyone."

For a long time after Mike Tyson uttered those words
to me I had been trying to absorb their meaning by
osmosis. I desperately wanted to feel the same way.
When I heard that Mike Tyson was about to embark
on a one-man Las Vegas stage show about his life,
back in the spring of 2012, I immediately tracked
down his public relations representative and threw
my hat into the ring for an interview. I had tried to
interview Mike in years past, but for a long while he
had shunned the press. From what I heard second
and third hand through people in the business, it
was because the media had still been trying to paint
him as this out-of-control thug, and he just didn't
feel that image accurately portrayed who he was
any longer.

It's always a great feeling when you've pitched
yourself to a publicist for an interview and then
out of the blue you get that phone call: "Hi, we
got your interview request. Are you still interested
in speaking with Mike?" All bets were off when he
was ready to promote his stage show, *Mike Tyson:
Undisputed Truth*. At the top of our interview I said
something like, "Thanks for taking the time to speak
with me today." That was something I always said to
my interview subjects because they were entrusting
me with their story, they were investing their time

with me, and I really *did* appreciate it. Mike giggled and said, "Hi Allison. Aww, c'mon, don't do that." He didn't want to be revered or looked at as superior in any way... at least not with me. He found my reverence towards him embarrassing, which I thought was quite sweet and endearing. Ironically, his attitude was much different in his boxing heyday. The first official question I asked him was if it was possible to be successful and happy at the same time. From my own experience, extreme prolific production in one's career usually coincides with lack of balance in one's personal life. Mike had once been quoted as saying that a person had to be willing to give up their happiness to achieve his level of success. I asked him if, in 2012 *(the year we spoke)*, that sentiment still rang true for him. Here's what he said:

> "Even when I had a billion dollars, I just wanted to do well. That's how I am. Sometimes in wanting to do well I have to block out any chances of being happy, because I want to accomplish a goal. That's how I've been raised by Cus D'Amato. Happiness is not worth your goal."

As we danced through different topics, there were moments when I laughed so hard, I thought my sides would split. Mike told me he was a big Judy Garland fan, and then went on to regale me with a story of his experience watching a particular performance of hers. I swear, the audio footage of this little monologue of his would make even the most despondent person laugh like no tomorrow! I'll admit I played it back to listen to it several times, as well as replaying it for some friends:

Allison Kugel: If Todd Phillips (writer & director of "The Hangover") came to you and said, "I have a role for you in my next film, not playing Mike Tyson, but a fictional role," what do you think you could bring to the table as an actor?

Mike Tyson: As an actor, he would get what Mike Tyson gave in the ring. He would get everything I have, and that's a lot. I'm that kind of extreme guy where I give it all or nothing. I want to die on stage and just give it all. That's the kind of guy I am. I'm a Judy Garland type of guy that wants to die on stage, and just go for it!

Allison Kugel (Laughs). Are you a Judy Garland fan?

Mike Tyson: Oh, explicitly! She's a beast! I was just watching [a film] last night where she was working with a bunch of mentally handicapped children with Burt Lancaster, and she's playing the piano. This is how much of a fan I am of hers; when I watch it I am looking at her and this is a moment when she is drinking a lot, and I'm watching her bloated and looking at her eyes and thinking, "This is her drinking period, now." She has the bloated eyes and face. But there is no doubt about it, she is just a *beast*! I saw a picture of her when they were talking about her life and they show her as a little girl. They put her up against another little girl and they were both singing at the same time, and she just ripped this other girl to shreds. The other girl was singing one of these zippidy-doo-da white songs, and [Judy] sang three different styles in one song. She started singing a basic white song... and then *boom*! She got on some pop, and *boom*! She started singing some R&B and she started scatting on this chick. She just ripped this little white girl to shreds! She's a *monster*! She did three styles in one song and started rippin' her.

Allison Kugel: (Laughs). Who would have thought, Mike Tyson loves Judy Garland.

Some other things I found interesting about Mike, when we spoke about his infamous marriage to actress Robin Givens, he referred to it as "an affair." He didn't utter the word "marriage." He also expressed that some of his richest years, monetarily speaking, were some of his saddest, and now with much less money to his name, he is happier.

Here's what he had to say about that:

Allison Kugel: What will the next ten years bring you?

Mike Tyson: I just hope life. If it brings life, then that's all I need.

Allison Kugel: Meaning, you no longer look to material things.

Mike Tyson: No, that's not what we're working on. We're working on art now. We're working on shows and our production company. We owe too much money to the government to ever be rich again, but you don't need money to be happy.

Speaking of anxiety, I thought he was going to have a conniption fit when he saw something happening to the pigeons on his property. If you doubted Mike Tyson's love for pigeons or thought it was just some weird PR stunt, you'd be wrong. A hawk began circling Mike's beloved pigeons and he began to freak out. We had to put our interview on hold for a bit while he tended to the pigeons and made sure they were all safe and sound.

A few months after speaking with Mike, I *wished* that pigeons were my sole source of angst. Little did I know how severe the grip of anxiety would prove to be in the coming months.

So where was I?

As the ER nurse and other assorted hospital staff ushered me into another room for an x-ray, and then back to my cubicle and cot, I felt an intense rush that came from my first experience of surrendering control to something outside of myself in quite a long time; in years really. My life had become a daily practice of taking control over my circumstances, my emotions, and my destiny. My need for control became insidious and slowly began to seep into every aspect of my life. I did not desire to ever be a passenger in a car when someone other than my immediate family was driving. I experienced an increasing dislike of airplanes. I developed an intense fear of the people around me dying and leaving me behind. I checked and re-checked food packages and medicine bottles to be sure they were all properly sealed, and I refused to ever let a loved one have the last word in an argument.

Control was the crux of my daily ritual for keeping anxiety at bay. This need to control my world and to not be a "victim of circumstance" as I often referred to it, was not all bad.

On the contrary, my Type-A personality *(mainly inherited from my paternal grandfather and my father–the Kugel bloodline)* allowed me the bravado and blind courage to start my own public relations business in 2003, to pioneer a thriving career as a journalist, and gave me the chutzpah to experience living in three different states: New York, California and Florida. Yes, I was my own person. No one was ever going to hold me back or, worse, tell me what to do. Not even God, Himself.

Little did I know, I was about to experience a large magnitude of change in every area of my life that would shake me to my core, have me question and then re-affirm my faith, break and re-build my body, and eventually re-acquaint me with my soul and with God…

Meghan McCain would be my very last interview ever published as a contracted Senior Editor of the newswire I was employed by. As often happens within companies, my then-editor wished for me to succeed… though not *too much*. And I wanted creative control, sometimes to the point of clear insubordination, I will admit. But any overt evidence that I had arrived as a force to be reckoned with in the media industry, apart from my media outlet, created some conflict. This matter is a point of contention between me and Jason, my former editor, to this day. Though a personal friendship was re-built and remains intact. If my name was mentioned in the press regarding an interview, I was accused of promoting myself rather than my media outlet. If I accepted an interview to discuss my career, accepted a freelance assignment *(which I was legally allowed to do)* or even pursued my own blog, I was, er, questioned. I knew I needed out and one day the camel's back broke and I simply said, "Fuck you, I quit."

That fateful resignation occurred on a morning in July of 2012 when I had just taken a conference call with one of the heads of marketing and public relations for the NBA. We had interviewed Shaquille O'Neal and Mike Tyson, but beyond those two, we hadn't really branched out into coverage of sports figures in the way I had wanted to. I hoped that this new relationship with the NBA would help to change that.

After a successful phone call that left me hopeful that we would begin to expand our journalism portfolio deeper into the world of professional sports, I picked up the phone and called my boss. I relayed the good news, to which he replied by telling me he wanted the person's contact information so that he could also see about doing some business deals with him. I hesitated and then blurted out, "No. I don't really think that's a good idea. Not right now. Let's establish things on the editorial side, first, before you approach them about any other business matters. Let's not confuse things right now."

My response was not favorable, and he interpreted it as a blatant act of insubordination on my part. Now, I'll admit that being someone's employee and listening to authority has not always been my strong suit. Okay, it never has. In fact, I am aware that I can be a bit of a, shall we say, renegade, when I am certain about my convictions. And my poor ex-boss; trying to wrangle and rope me in was like trying to hogtie a pig dipped in oil. It just wasn't going to happen. Like the way comedienne Tina Fey did that Sarah Palin bit on *Saturday Night Live*, where she declared in her best mock Alaskan accent, "This is where I go rogue." Yea, I've been known to go rogue. But hey, how the hell else do you think I managed to even accrue all these interviews? Playing by the rules? It's a package deal. I never claimed to be docile and go-with-the-flow. We now joke about it, because I now come to him with the headaches and grievances that come along with being an employer and I get the old, "I told you so." Touché. Life is like a prism. We need to experience seeing through all sides of the prism to achieve a well-rounded human experience.

After some back and forth arguing, my editor lost his temper and shouted, "This is my company! I'm the dictator and you do what I say!" I can remember the word "dictator" like it was yesterday. Some people make great friends but lousy co-workers. One thing that drove me a little nuts was being called on the weekends and expected to drop everything during a family outing, even though there really was no emergency. It was odd, to be honest. I couldn't get a grasp on what was going on at the time. It began to tear away at the fabric of my happiness and my health. And the weirdest part of it all? Now that we're great friends again and we no longer work together, the guy never calls me on the weekend.

Now, Jason, my former editor, is a pretty gentle type of a guy in his everyday life. He's the kind of guy who would probably tear up during a Hallmark commercial if the moment was just right. You have to understand, tensions had been mounting in our working relationship for quite some time; years really. We were both to blame.

It was a real tooth-and-nail scenario, and by this particular summer day we had really had it with each other. During our eight years working together, we did the impossible. We moved mountains. We created something amazing. But we also drove each other fucking nuts. At the time it was very painful and I would often suffer from stomachaches, headaches and just feeling downright stressed because of our epic blowouts. In retrospect, I am wise enough to know that it takes two to tango, and our personalities and sensibilities just clashed at that particular time in our history.

I got off the phone after the "NBA fight" and I had the shakes. I felt ill. I felt, "This just isn't worth it anymore." I had to do one of the hardest things I'd ever had to do. I had to walk away from the best job of my life; something I'd birthed and raised from infancy. And I walked away empty handed.

And so it goes…

No two weeks' notice. No goodbye party. No sticking around to help find my replacement. Just, "Fuck you, I quit." I think a lot of people fantasize about saying that if they won the lottery or something. I didn't win the lottery, but life is short. I jumped without a parachute and hoped for the best.

Without discussing any more of the details surrounding my, *ahem*, resignation, let's just say it was time to move on.

I suffered that classic boomerang effect shortly after my dramatic and abrupt departure from a website that I helped build, and I fell into a deep depression. My depression at losing something I helped to create, heaped on top of the anxiety that I was already suffering took its toll on me. I knew that doing these interviews was not just a job, but my life's work. It had become my creative and emotional outlet. I began to mourn the loss of it as if it were a death.

A few days later a bright light came in the form of an unexpected email I got from character actor, Joe Pantoliano, aka Joey Pants. Joe's acting career took an iconic turn with his Emmy winning portrayal of Ralph Cifaretto on *The Sopranos*…

I had originally interviewed Joe on-camera in December of 2010 about his own struggles with anxiety, depression, OCD and addiction. That interview had taken place in Joe's publicist's office with my then camera crew filming the conversation.

During that 2010 face-to-face interview, Joe and I discovered that we shared the same birthday, September 12th.

During our sit down, I listened to Joe recount stories from his episodes of acute anxiety and depression, and I silently commiserated and related quite easily. Though at the time I was in great spirits and my own demons had not been acting up. Joe's, on the other hand, seemed to be outwardly manifested right out in front of me. It was right before Christmas and everyone was already mentally on vacation. I was in my seat, body mic in place, lights up and burning through my heavily made up skin. The camera guys were staring into space and checking their watches when Joe finally came blowing through the door and into the room where we were all waiting for his arrival. Frankly, he didn't look well. He was perspiring heavily and seemed out of sorts. He took his seat across from mine and began dabbing at his brow with a handkerchief.

When the makeup artist, a friend of mine, Filis Forman, came over to powder him up he shooed her away. "I go without makeup," he insisted. He was trying to gather himself and recounted that he'd been running late shooting some project and had jumped on the subway to make it to our interview. "The subway was really hot and stuffy, and I'm just really tired." I glanced over at Joe's publicist, Brad Taylor, and over at the head camera guy, Paul Brozen. "Are you alright to do this?" I asked Joe. I was concerned. At the end of the day we're all human beings. I wouldn't want someone to go through a forty-five minute on-camera inquisition if they are feeling ill. I mean, if anyone could empathize, it was me.

Joe was a trooper. "No, I'll be alright. I just need to relax," he said. "Ok, let's get the show on the road then," I quipped, and motioned over to Paul to start shooting. I just wanted to get it done so the poor guy could go home. I rearranged my own posture into professional journalist position; straight-backed, leaning slightly forward, note cards in hand, but low enough as to not ruin the shot…

Fast forward to July of 2012 and I received an email from Joe who was reaching out to let me know that he came upon the print version of our 2010 interview together. He wanted to know if I would be interested in speaking with him again, this time to help him promote his latest book, *Asylum: Hollywood Tales from My Great Depression: Brain Dis-Ease, Recovery, and Being My Mother's Son*. It was a follow up to his New York Times best-selling memoir, *Who's Sorry Now (E P Dutton, October 2002)*. He sounded a hell of a lot better than he did two years before; great in fact.

I picked up the phone and called Joey to say hello. We chatted for a bit. He told me that he had never read our first interview together until just a few days prior and he really loved it, and wanted to do something together again. He told me all about his new book, *Asylum*, and what topics he wanted to cover in our second interview. I told him that I was no longer at my cushy contracted gig, and was now "freelancing," but that I would use my connections to get excerpts from the second interview syndicated throughout online media. We made an appointment to talk later that week and I got to work reading his new book. It gave me a pinhole of light at the end of a long dark tunnel. I realized that maybe my career wasn't over and I could dust myself off and re-brand myself as an independent syndicated journalist. In any event, I was happy for the distraction of work to see me through until my upcoming appointment with a psychiatrist from Weill Cornell Hospital in New York, who could hopefully cure what was ailing me.

Like any disease that resides in the brain, whether it is anxiety and panic disorder, depression, addiction or an eating disorder, the sufferer is often misunderstood and isolated. Friends and family make their best attempts at sympathy and even empathy, though they simply don't know what it feels like to be inside your skin. Many of these brain "dis-*eases*," as actor Joe Pantoliano calls it, are a perfect storm of brain chemistry meeting some kind of emotional trigger that enables the dis-*ease* to manifest. It's like striking a match, if you will. You can have the match and the contact paper, but if you don't rub them together in the right way, no fire. But once you strike the match to rough textured paper, you have fire. People with a pre-disposition to anxiety and panic disorder exist with a match and a matchbook in hand at all times. Certain unfavorable circumstances are metaphoric to that match tip rubbing against the matchbook. Once the proverbial fire is ignited it takes a fair amount of work to put it out.

When the day of my second interview with Joe Pantoliano arrived, I felt a certain comfort at knowing I would be interviewing someone who has been down a similar path as me. I didn't feel the need to conceal my current emotional state. In fact, I was kind of upfront about it throughout our conversation. Rather than being a blank slate to his colorful personal declarations, I piped up and told him that I was currently suffering from chronic panic attacks and was having a hell of a time with it. His response was, "You're so normal, Allison." That one response stays with me because it made me feel like less of a freak, and it felt good to just say it: "I have an anxiety disorder, and I'm not well right now." It was what it was.

At the time, before some business complications set in, I was running my own fledgling blog, AllisonsWord. com, and it was beginning to pick up steam much to the chagrin of my former employer. Throughout this interview with Joe he told me how he was champing at the bit to win a guest starring role on the Aaron Sorkin produced HBO series, *The Newsroom*. He also mentioned to me how he had overheard at an industry luncheon *The Real Housewives of Beverly Hills* former cast member Taylor Armstrong complain that her *People* Magazine cover had been thwarted by the passing of the late singer, Amy Winehouse.

I put my contacts to work and we generated a lot of press around the web for those two stories, in particular. I hit up my interview syndicator, W.E.N.N. (World Entertainment News Network) with the initial instinct to credit the stories to my own name, Allison Kugel. I was then talked into crediting my blog, the now defunct AllisonsWord.com. My instincts told me I needed to brand my name but it was one of those rare moments when I ignored my inner voice. Bad move. Live and Learn. Here are a few samples of the pick-ups Joe and I received throughout the online media space:

Yahoo omg! UK

Actor Joe Pantoliano is desperate to work with Aaron Sorkin on his new TV drama The Newsroom, insisting he would happily work in the catering department just to see the screenwriter/producer in action.

The series, which stars Jeff Daniels as a highly-strung veteran newscaster, has received mixed reviews since debuting in June, but Pantoliano admits he's hooked on the show and would do anything to land a job on the programme.

The Sopranos star tells AllisonsWord.com, "I've got this thing for Aaron Sorkin and The Newsroom. I would work craft services on that.

I just love how his mind works, and how prolific he is as a writer. I would do it in a heartbeat."

Express.co.uk

Joe Pantoliano not a fan of reality TV

Former THE SOPRANOS star JOE PANTOLIANO has taken aim at his fellow Americans over their obsession with reality TV.

Published: Sat, August 11, 2012

The actor insists shows like *The Real Housewives* and *Keeping Up With the Kardashians* set a bad example for the youth of today and contribute to the "societal decline" of the U.S.

He tells blog AllisonsWord.com, "I don't watch it (reality TV). I think it's really damaging. I think it's another nail in the coffin of this societal decline. (Reality) television caters to the lowest denomination. If it's being viewed, it doesn't have anything to do with content.

"It promotes the kind of insidious, self-centered, narcissistic horses**t like The Real Housewives.

"Now what do these kids think? These kids are thinking, 'Oh, I'll be a reality star. Or do a sex tape and leak it out and become a star.' You got to be careful showing these kids that stuff. I have a real pet peeve about that."

Pantoliano sparked a feud with Real Housewives regular Taylor Armstrong earlier this week (beg06Aug12) when he recalled overhearing her at a charity party allegedly complaining about how Amy Winehouse's death had bumped her off the front of America's People magazine.

Armstrong's publicist insists her client would never have made the comments the actor claims he heard.

Gather.com
Taylor Armstrong Attacked by a 'Soprano'

Filed in Gather Celeb News Channel by Lindsay Cronin on August 10, 2012

Taylor Armstrong is in a bitter feud with Joe Pantoliano, star of *The Sopranos*, after he claims the *Real Housewives of Beverly Hills* star had some not-so-nice things to say about Amy Winehouse's death—and the suicide of her husband, Russell Armstrong.

Joe claims he overheard Taylor complaining about how she was bumped off the cover of *People* Magazine by the news of Amy Winehouse's untimely death. She had planned to do a cover and in depth interview about her late husband's passing, but Winehouse's death reigned supreme.

In an interview with AllisonsWord.com, Joe claimed, "There she was, having breakfast across the way from me. You could see she had all of this work done, and she was complaining how Amy Winehouse knocked her off the cover of People magazine because she up and died, and that she would have gotten the cover because her husband committed suicide. Not kidding you."

Taylor's rep has responded and says, "She's (Taylor) incredibly insulted by this false accusation. It is also impossible that this would have been the case since Amy Winehouse died almost a month before Russell, and therefore Amy would have been on the cover when Russell was still alive and well." She adds, "It is shocking that Mr. Pantoliano would say this, as it is extremely morbid and makes light of the death of both Taylor's husband and Miss Winehouse."

Here's my sidebar on former RHOBH star Taylor Armstrong

In case you're wondering, Joe's account of what he heard from Taylor Armstrong was true, though I think his memory might have confused some of the particulars. It wouldn't surprise me at all that Taylor would have been gunning for a cover story when she was promoting her memoir about her marriage to late husband, Russell Armstrong, and his suicide. In reality, it's not because she is a bad or unfeeling person. Business is business, and when you are promoting a book, specifically a memoir, the cover of *People* is a huge coup. She and her team were probably bummed that the Amy Winehouse story took precedence over her story. Sounds shallow, but when you are in that business, you kind of get it. You're fighting to make a space for yourself in a saturated market and you need all of the press and hype you can get. Though at first blush I told Joe that it was disgusting for Taylor to complain about that, if I'm being completely honest, I would have wanted the cover too.

Feeling Existential in 2015.

CHAPTER TWO

"There is no such thing as me or mine. There is only us."
- told to me by Deepak Chopra

Ahhh, the gurus. I've often joked by saying, "How does one become a guru? Is there a specific major you can take in college for that?" I've interviewed several of the world's experts on health, wellness and spirituality over the years; Dr. Deepak Chopra, Dr. Andrew Weil, Dr. Sanjay Gupta... people whom the world looks to for answers. I was honored to have a private front row seat to pick their brains. I admire all of these men. Their contributions to the world and their depth of intellect and higher mindfulness keeps me stimulated and thinking.

When I booked the interview with Deepak Chopra I was honored to have his private time and I swear it was surreal to hear the outgoing message on his cell phone voicemail. I think it was something simple like, "This is Deepak, please leave a message," but it felt like the closest thing to calling God's cell phone and hearing his personal voicemail. So when

I dialed him up to chat and got his voicemail I was actually happy to leave a message. "Hi Dr. Chopra. It's Allison Kugel. We are supposed to speak at such and such time. Give me a call back at –––––." Wow! Did I just leave a voicemail for Deepak Chopra?! I'm not made of stone. It was pretty fucking cool.

Speaking with Dr. Chopra came at a time when I was just beginning to delve into matters of the spirit world, quantum physics, and becoming cognizant of something existing outside of the realm of our five senses. It was January of 2008. I had just completed reading several books by Dr. Brian Weiss, which go into topics of past life regression, reincarnation, communication with Master Spirits, and the universe beyond earth's physical plane. I always keep copies of Dr. Weiss' bestseller, *Many Lives, Many Masters*, on hand and regularly give copies out as gifts to friends. To this day, spiritual matters that transcend the physical world remains my favorite topic of study. And like everyone else and their mother, I watched *The Secret* in 2006. It woke up an eagerness within me to learn more. But speaking with Deepak Chopra was the first I'd ever heard of the concept of time being an illusion that exists only here in the physical world, in the collective minds of human beings.

Here is an excerpt from our conversation, and I have been thinking about it ever since:

Allison Kugel: And the concept of time as being an illusion?

Deepak Chopra: Well, if you're in love then time doesn't exist. If you're having a good time, it flies. If you're having deadlines then you start to think, "I'm running out of time." If you're bored you say, "Time is dragging." If you're in a very anxious situation, then time takes forever. Time is the way we measure our experience. In the deeper domains where there is unity consciousness, time doesn't exist. Time is the movement of thought. It separates the observer from the observed when in the deepest reality, the observer and the observed, the seer and the scenery, the lover and the beloved… they're all the same consciousness.

At first blush some of you might dismiss this as crunchy granola eating, tree hugging nonsense. But I urge you to transcend that initial reaction and ponder the true meaning of time, or the lack thereof. And I get it; if you're late for work, telling your boss to relax because time doesn't really exist ain't gonna fly. It's true that here on this physical plane where we currently reside, we do have to observe and obey the concept of earthly time, but we don't have to be *trapped* in time by the human mind and the ego. We can distance ourselves from the concept of time whenever we are afforded the practical ability to do so.

Another question begging to be asked was how to make sense of the discrepancies between the "brain self" and the "soul self." In other words, supposing someone is suffering from mental illness or mental impairment. Is this coming from a compromised brain or a compromised soul? Where does one end and the other begin? Here's another excerpt from my conversation with Deepak Chopra that is worth noting. It certainly cleared this one up for me:

Allison Kugel: How do you determine, according to your understanding, what you would refer to as the soul or the spirit, and the brain? In other words, when that inner voice speaks to us or when we are having certain thoughts or feelings, what is coming from our soul and what is coming from our brain?

Deepak Chopra: Everything comes from the soul. The brain is an instrument. All your fears, all your anxieties, all your phobias, all your imagination, all your fantasies, all your desires, your creativity, your insight, your intuition, your inspiration, your conflicts... the soul is a place of extreme opposites. It's a place of ambiguity, a place of uncertainty, and a place of contradiction and paradox. The brain is just the instrument which orchestrates what your soul is. Your soul is evolving. It starts from a place of extreme ignorance and ultimately ends up in a place of extreme enlightenment. That's our journey. We use our brain and our body to orchestrate everything.

Allison Kugel: But, if you take somebody like a mental health practitioner, and you were to bring up the topics of bipolar disorder, anxiety, depression, phobias, they would argue that it comes from chemical reactions taking place in the brain. Do you disagree?

Deepak Chopra: Well, if I am listening to Beethoven on my radio and my radio is damaged, I won't be able to hear Beethoven until I fix the radio. They're right. You have to fix the instrument. But the fault of the instrument is not a reflection of the user of the instrument.

In March of 2012 I was privileged to speak with an expert on that very instrument; Neurosurgeon and CNN Medical Correspondent, Dr. Sanjay Gupta.

Dr. Gupta had recently published a novel, *Monday Mornings*, which takes the reader inside the secretive Monday morning Morbidity & Mortality meetings that many teaching hospitals conduct each week. In Morbidity & Mortality meetings taking place in hospitals across the country, hospital administrators review and dissect medical mistakes that took place at the hospital the week prior; some which may have even led to patient mortality. It's not a pleasant thing to think about, the fact that doctors are human and they do occasionally make fatal errors. In fact, analyzing medical errors is actually one of the practices by which physicians improve and refine their skills, and breadth of knowledge. I found this to be a frightening yet incredibly fascinating dichotomy. When it comes to reading, I am typically a non-fiction fan, though I devoured the pages of Dr. Gupta's novel, *Monday Mornings*.

When my interview with Dr. Sanjay Gupta started he was huffing and puffing away on his treadmill and he apologized for multitasking. As we discussed various themes relating to the brain and medicine, I took note of a certain pattern of development in my recent body of work. I was definitely attempting to decode the dance of human anatomy and spiritual anatomy. Here is a line of questioning that I found pretty interesting:

Allison Kugel: As a neurosurgeon and a scientist you've studied every facet of the human brain from motor skills and memory to addiction and disease. That being said, do you believe that we have a soul, or do you believe that we are merely organic computers?

Dr. Sanjay Gupta: I don't think I've ever been asked that before. That's a good question. I guess I've always believed people have a soul, and that's not something that I could subjectively prove. What's the old saying that scientists use? "In God we trust. Everyone else bring data."   There's no data on this one. But to me it's inconceivable that there isn't more than a bunch of carbon that comprises us as human beings. Exactly what to call the other thing, whether it's a soul or something else, what it's made of or where it goes, I don't know. But my simple answer to the question is I think we have a soul in the way that you're describing it.

Allison Kugel: Aside from scientific evidence, throughout your travels as a physician have you come across anecdotal evidence that you've filed away in the back of your mind?

Dr. Sanjay Gupta: Do you know what the word, teleological, means? It basically means when an outcome has occurred you try and work it backwards to explain it. For example, in the religion of Hinduism there is this belief that there is a Nirvana. Nirvana means an absolution of all worldly things, and that you're ready to move on to whatever is the next thing. It was kind of crunchy granola stuff for me when it was explained to me as a scientist. When you see deaths that are completely inexplicable, like in a young kid or just some horrible, horrible death, you think to yourself, "Why would that happen? How could any justification in our universe possibly let that

> happen?" And then you think to yourself that
> if there is such a thing as Nirvana, this idea that
> someone has achieved a sense of inner peace
> and they are actually ready to be absolved of
> earthly attachments, then perhaps that could
> explain it.

During our chat he told me that television veteran producer David E. Kelley was turning his novel into a television series that would be titled, *Chelsea General*, the name of the fictional hospital in Dr. Gupta's novel, *Monday Mornings*. Always one to speak my mind, I said, "Really? I kind of like the idea of the show being called *Monday Mornings,* just like the book." Gupta commiserated, saying, "I know, I know. I felt the same way. But they really want to call it *Chelsea General*, because what if the show doesn't get a Monday timeslot? I was told it would then confuse people as to when it's on."

I don't know if Dr. Gupta took my temperature and reported the conversation back to the producers, but the show did air with the title *Monday Mornings*. I watched the first few episodes and felt it was a compelling premise with a stellar cast that wasn't given enough of a chance by the network that aired it, TNT.

As of May 2012 I was living the dream, as I knew my dream to be at the time. I was self-employed with my own established public relations firm, I had another full time career as a celebrity journalist where my weekly duties involved interviewing famous people. I lived in a beautiful four bedroom house in sunny Florida with my son, Marcus, my significant other, Patrick, and our Shih tzu, Frankie. We spent our weekends on some of Florida's most picturesque beaches, I still had three living grandparents that I visited regularly, and sometimes a day's work would involve laying under a palm tree as I read the memoir of the latest person I was scheduled to interview. I know, I know. Rough life!

On a typically glorious south Florida morning during the spring of 2012, I can recall standing in my center-island kitchen, coffee cup in hand, watching my then boyfriend, my three year old son, and our dog playing and laughing. A smile swept across my face. I can clearly recall thinking, "I am so blessed. I feel as though I am living in an idyllic sitcom version of my own life." Suddenly, as I was often prone to doing, I began to have thoughts that things seemed too perfect, too peaceful, and that the other shoe was sure to drop. I shrugged it off as my true-to-form Type-A neurosis and continued to revel in my own existence. Suddenly the house phone rang and in my boyfriend's pokerfaced fashion, he uttered stoically into the phone, "Uh-huh, ok, ok then. Bye." He sounded eerily calm, in fact. I knew something was up.

"What was *that* all about?" I thought. As even and steady as always, Patrick stated, "That was your father. Your parents are on their way down to Florida and your dad wants you to go to the hospital. Your Nanny *(my lifelong affectionate name for my paternal grandmother)* is in the hospital, but she should be ok." Hmm, something inside of me suddenly shifted uncomfortably. I suspected all was not ok. I was right. My precious, beautiful grandmother whom I looked up to and adored my entire life had suffered a massive stroke that would create a significant enough bleed inside of her brain that her mind and faculties would never return. Though her physical body was still of this earth, in essence, my Nanny was gone. Just like that. And to make matters worse, the last time I spent with the lucid version of her was at a dinner where my son, then two, was acting up to the point where the restaurant's maître de asked us to leave. My son was in rare form that evening and I was so exasperated that I gave Nanny a quick distracted hug goodbye and turned my attention back to my disorderly son as we got into the car and drove home. Had I only known that half-hearted hug would be our last true hug...

This would be the beginning of a shakeup in my life so significant that I would never return to that place of complete bliss again, figuratively or literally, for quite some time.

For weeks, mine and my boyfriend's schedules, and even that of our son, would revolve making weekly trips to a nursing home about forty miles south of our home in Palm Beach County. I would hug and kiss Nanny and witness her deterioration from a vibrant and glamorous woman to an elderly, helpless woman who needed assistance to do even the most basic tasks.

She no longer remembered my son whom she once doted on, and I could feel the effect it had on him. I resolved on one such trip that it would not be emotionally healthy for my son to return. All the while, Patrick was loving and supportive, doing all that he could to help my grandmother and reassure my father and me.

In the midst of this trauma I received a phone call from my parents. They told us they were canceling a planned trip down to Florida to spend time with us because my father had not performed adequately during a stress test given to him by his cardiologist, and that the matter had to be investigated further. Anyone who knows my father knows that he is a patriarch in the truest sense of the word. Richard Kugel is the type of figure that has you convinced that as long as he is around no harm will come to you, and all will be right in the world. Having built an extremely successful tire distributorship from scratch, successfully providing for my mother, myself and my two brothers, and thinking on his feet to create the most favorable outcome in any scenario, we always felt safe with my father as a presence in our everyday lives. He was our rock.

My father has lived with various ailments for as long as I can remember, including juvenile Type-1 Diabetes which he inherited from Nanny, liver disease and a thyroid condition. Somehow or another he has managed to remain strong in our eyes and his yearly physicals with his various specialists and primary care physician were always good. I never would have expected that my father would fall prey to heart disease. Before I could fully process what was going on, my dad was going into the hospital for an angiogram. His angiogram was swiftly followed by having several stents placed in his severely clogged arteries.

According to the cardiologist, my father was a ticking time bomb with his main artery, nicknamed "the widow-maker" by cardiologists, being ninety-five percent clogged. These stents were put in place just in the nick of time.

To say that I was spooked by what *could* have been is a gross understatement. Between my grandmother and my father, life was beginning to seem less idyllic and I was now on high alert.

My personal terror thermometer blasted upwards from yellow to a screaming red. I felt the foundation beneath my feet begin to loosen and rock back and forth. Things were changing and I was not happy.

On June 9, 2012 Patrick, our son Marcus, and I arrived in New York for what was supposed to be a summer vacation up north. We would take in some

Broadway musicals, eat at a few of our favorite restaurants, catch up with old friends and visit all of our old haunts in the area. "Marcus would adjust just fine to a two-state lifestyle," I thought. He could go to camp on Long Island and go to school during the year at home in Florida. A very glamorous and progressive lifestyle. Fail! Kids don't think that way, particularly three-year-olds.

After about two and a half weeks in New York, my son began to crack as he wondered why we were on such an extended vacation and why he couldn't be back at home in Florida with his things, his dog and his friends. "I'm done with grandma and grandpa and New York," he protested. "I'm ready to go back to Florida. I miss my friends." Patrick and I mulled over the idea of scrapping our extended summer stay and hightailing it back to Florida for our son. But soon enough he got into a routine at summer camp, while things between Patrick and I began to unravel. We were in no position to make the trip together back down south. In fact, we were in real trouble, but more about that later.

On the career front …

Conducting an interview independently and getting coverage for it felt like a tiny win, but it would be a solid year before my inner light came back on and I really began to move in the direction of complete re-invention. In that emergency room hospital bed in the summer of 2012 I was still far from ok.

As I continued to lay in the hospital in my tranquilized state, I felt the tension leave my body and my mind, though there was a part of me that continued to hold court with an ongoing inner dialogue.

The inner voice that wouldn't quit was not the product of my heavily sedated mind, but was coming from somewhere else. When your worldly faculties are compromised you become acquainted with another mechanism that resides inside of you. It exists apart from the mechanics of your brain and your body, and seems to inexplicably operate independent of your physical self. I have always recognized this as my soul, my inner being. You can call it whatever you'd like. This voice is the greatest and most honest compass I possess in this life. I trust it implicitly.

The little voice inside of me that remained completely clear through my fog of medication took me on a journey from childhood through present day, and showed me a portrait of a little girl and then a woman who has always been bound and driven by fear. My whole life up until that point had, in fact, been an exercise in avoiding situations where I would not be in the driver's seat. Granted, several of my less than favorable experiences throughout my life happened when I was not in control of my circumstances. Unfavorable things would always seem to occur when I was caught off-guard, thus setting up a fail-safe system in me where I would always keep one eye on potential trouble up ahead and one eye on whatever it was I was actually doing in the moment.

Me and dad in Florida c. 1975.

Posing in my living room c. 1981.

Me and mom in Florida c. 1974.

Me and mom at the park c. 1977.

With my Grandpa Larry and Papa Morty (holding me) at my brother David's bris in February 1979.

Interestingly enough, both good and bad things had happened throughout my life with an extra wrinkle; a healthy helping of anxiety threaded throughout. It managed to ruin countless days of my life.

Whether waiting for blood test results, awaiting news regarding the fate of a loved one, or waiting to hear about a particular career opportunity, my modus operandi was to torture myself until I received my answer. I became addicted to that feeling of sweet release once I was given good news.

The panic attacks, obsessive compulsive rituals, they had come to a head and were no longer my shield of protection. They threatened to undo me.

CHAPTER THREE

"It's about the music. For me, it all boils down to the music."
- told to me by Nancy Sinatra

I was born on September 12, 1974, just as the Sears Tower was being erected in Chicago, pocket calculators adorned mathematicians everywhere, and scientists were discovering and regulating pollution in our drinking water. Growing up, times were relatively simple. I listened to eight-tracks of Neil Sedaka and the soundtrack to the movie *Grease* in my parents' living room. Luxury cars were the size of small boats and digital technology wasn't even a glimmer in Steve Jobs' eye.

Compared to our world today, which moves at lightning speed with real danger lurking in all corners of our earth, my generation enjoyed a feeling of relative safety and a state of innocence that my own son will never know. Yet, from the time I was old enough to walk, talk, and recognize my place on this planet, I can recall a constant inner companion that made me feel just a little frightened and tentative much of the time.

That unwelcome companion grew in strength as I began to grow up. Now I can label it "anxiety," though I didn't know what to call it at the time. I was a very intuitive, sensitive and introspective child and always felt slightly out of step with others my own age. Generally speaking, my preference was to be in the company of my parents' and my grandparents' contemporaries. I felt they understood the world better and had more important things to share with me. I seemed to recognize myself as an old soul with a strong inner dialogue. I often wondered if other kids my age would confer with that silent inner voice that felt as palpable to me as any physical being. Because of this sensitivity and proclivity towards hyper-awareness, I developed an early tendency to over-empathize with others. If I knew of someone suffering from a physical illness, I too would develop the symptoms of that illness and imagine that I was living those circumstances, much to my own detriment.

At the age of eight, my friend Denise's older sister, Renee, who couldn't have been more than two or three years older than Denise and I, was diagnosed with an in-operable brain tumor. This was my first realization of mortality and the notion that being young does not guarantee invincibility. I was close with Denise and I watched in silent horror as her older sister Renee deteriorated further and further each time I went over to Denise's house to play. Finally, at the age of thirteen, Renee passed away. I was dumbfounded and utterly traumatized by receiving the news that she had died. I begged and pleaded with my mother to not make me go back to Denise's house ever again, as I could not face the reality of her older sister's untimely demise. But when Denise was having her eighth birthday party, my mother insisted that I go.

Shortly after that I began to develop disturbing headaches and various other bodily sensations that I was convinced were the symptoms of a brain tumor. I immediately feared that I would meet the same fate as Renee, and I began to panic at the thought of losing control over my body. I felt alone and vulnerable. This was my first glimpse into the abyss of anxiety and phobias. At age eight I had no skills to process what I was experiencing, nor the ability to fend it off.

About a year later, my parents, who met and were married in short order, inside of seven months, both at the tender age of twenty-one, began to fight as a matter of routine. They didn't seem to try to make any effort at hiding their marital discord from my little brother, David, and me. Each Sunday seemed to hold the same fate. My mother would get me and my younger brother dressed for "family day" whereby she chose some organized activity that the four of us could do together. As the morning wore on, she and my father would begin to argue over his frenetic work schedule, his lack of sensitivity toward her, his gambling or all three. The arguing would rise to a fever pitch, my mother would call my father every name in the book, and my father would take off in his car to blow off steam. His favorite place to unwind was the racetrack or OTB *(off-track betting)*. My five-year-old brother, David, and I would be standing there like two abandoned animals left by the side of the road as my mother let out a round of expletives before retiring to her bedroom.

All of this tumult led me to further withdraw and sink into my own mind where I developed a rich internal life that left little room for extroverted relationships or social activities. I felt most at home around in my own thoughts, as confusing and overwhelming as they were.

I retreated into a creative space in my mind, which became my home. I would imagine a more glamorized version of my own life, and I became fascinated by learning about other people's lives to fill in the blanks where my own experiences left off. I can remember cracking open the first biography I ever read. The year was 1988 and I was in my middle school Introduction to Computers class. When the teacher wasn't looking, I'd peel open this little paperback unauthorized biography about Madonna and peep a few pages before shoving the abridged book back into my folder so as not to be caught. When the bell rang and I finally had a lunch break, I ate quickly and used the remainder of my free time sitting in the school library devouring that book. I was so completely enthralled by the journey of reading and learning about someone else's life. I've been hooked ever since. Learning about someone's life, what they've gone through, what they have endured, learned, and then achieved, it just does it for me. Though, on that winter day in that middle school library in 1988 I hadn't known that one day I would be interviewing people for a living, for a decade of my life.

Sure, I was given little inklings and hints along the way but the best way for me to sum up my reaction to the universe when these sign posts came along the highway was, "Duh." It just didn't click. No matter what job I had throughout my twenties, from menial errand girl gigs that paid hourly wages to full time underling jobs, I was always told I could write. Subsequently, any and all writing work was dumped on me to complete. I can recall one particular moment in the year 2000. I was 25 years old. I was sitting in my apartment with my then-boyfriend, and mulling over what my life had in store for me. I was not exactly making much headway in any particular career, or financially-speaking. I was really sort of… lost. My boyfriend said what at the time I thought seemed hair-brained and unrealistic. "I know what would be perfect for you, Allison. You could talk to all of the celebrities, and interview them and write about them. You would be good at that."

I think I retorted with something like, "Thanks babe, great idea. And after that I could fly to the moon." It's not that I was a negative Nancy, it's just that it seemed far-fetched. I was a Criminal Justice major in college, I had no journalism experience of any kind, no contacts to speak of, and the Internet was far from the media juggernaut that it is today. It just seemed like a silly and random idea. It wasn't until I was a few years deep into my journalism career, one night when I was editing an interview into the wee hours of the morning, that old conversation came back to me and I smiled. It was a glimpse into the mystery and divinity of the universe, and that's why the smile spread across my face. I would come to have a lot of moments like that. You know those moments when a bunch of loose puzzle pieces that didn't seem to make sense all of a sudden fit together perfectly? Now, if you Google me, one of Google's search phrase suggestions that comes up is "Allison Kugel Interview." Cool, eh?

Soon I began to feel ill-at-ease around my peers and I reveled in playing hooky from school. I would come up with all sorts of ways to get my mother to keep me home from school. I even mastered a way to fake a temperature by running the thermometer under warm water and then popping it back under my tongue before my mother could catch on. Looking back, my self-esteem was low. Socially and academically, I just didn't want to have to measure up. It seemed easier to keep my mother company during the day.

I'd watch her run errands, meet with friends to fill her day with idle chatter about the goings on in our small community, and sit with her and her friends as they played mahjongg tiles or card games. I also loved the old television programs that were on during school hours, like re-runs of *I Love Lucy*, *Leave it to Beaver*, *The Love Boat* and *The Brady Bunch*. I even enjoyed shows from the 1950s like *Mr. Ed* and *My Three Sons*.

"Life seemed so much simpler and more pleasant back then," I would silently muse.

I also found a sense of peace in our frequent family trips to Florida to visit all four of my grandparents, especially my father's parents whom I affectionately called Nanny and Papa. My Nanny *(Thelma Ugelow Kugel)* was a glamorous woman whose coiffed blonde hair, makeup, designer clothing and perfume were always impeccable, and she adored me. Nanny and Papa lived in a sprawling 5,000 square foot ranch-style home with custom furnishings and accoutrements right out of *Architectural Digest* magazine. In fact, their home was even published in an issue of *Architectural Digest*; a proud moment for them as they were both eastern-European Jewish immigrants who grew up in tenement buildings in Brooklyn.

My Nanny's private bathroom was as large as a decent-sized bedroom, and her walk-in closet looked like a clothing boutique. She was my very own version of Elizabeth Taylor, and I was awed by her. Trips to Nanny and Papa's house were always full of excitement, from the plane ride down to Florida to the frequent lunches and swims at their country club. As a child, their home was the one place where I always felt special.

However, I can recall one such trip to Florida when I was feeling a bit fatigued and I broke out with some unexplained black and blue bruises all over my legs. My mind immediately flashed to something I had seen on television about pediatric Leukemia and I became convinced, once again, that the end was near. I worried and cried. I spoke to my grandparents and parents about my fear that I was dying of Leukemia as I pointed to the medical evidence on my marked up legs. A later trip to the pediatrician back in New York would give me a much simpler diagnosis. I had low levels of vitamin C, and I was put on a vitamin supplement.

Let me stop right here. If you aren't an anxiety sufferer with one of the hallmark manifestations, acute hypochondria, allow me to explain how the mind cycle of an anxiety sufferer works:

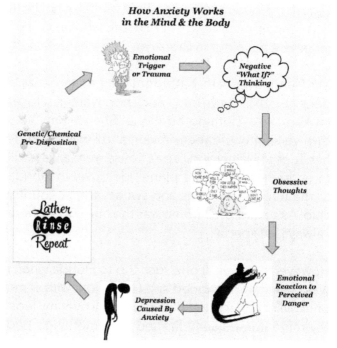

How Anxiety Works in the Mind & the Body

The above cycle of mind/body activity may seem alien to someone who does not suffer with anxiety and panic disorder. But at second glance it almost resembles the Stanislavsky method of acting that has won some of your favorite performers countless Oscar nominations and statuettes. And as long and drawn out as the above diagram appears, it trips off like a row of dominos being knocked down in a matter of seconds. It only takes seconds for the brain's amygdale *(the portion of the brain responsible for this reaction)* to create a five alarm fire of anxiety.

The mind of an anxiety sufferer is very much like that of a method actor. Our sense memory recall, empathic abilities and imaginations can go into overdrive, and stay there, without the proper tools. Call it a talent, a defect, or a direct line plugged into the collective human consciousness. It is what I jokingly call the four houseguests from hell-anxiety, panic, depression and OCD. You might be thinking, "You wouldn't let bad houseguests back into your home. Why would you allow them to take up residency in your mind?" If you're wired like I am and you haven't contemplated that obvious question, chew on it for a bit.

I once sat in on a method acting class in New York City where the teacher instructed all of us to close our eyes and visualize the tart taste of a lemon so completely that we would actually recoil as we pretended to bite into the lemon.

I remember thinking, "This is so silly." Now, ask me to visualize dying from an unthinkably heinous disease or perishing in a train wreck, and I've got that nailed. In fact, I've already prepared my acceptance speeches for those performances.

Getting back to my childhood fantasies, I often wonder why I didn't use that energy to fantasize about more positive things. If there is a permanent "what if...."? dialogue going on in my mind, filling in the blanks to that precarious phrase never leans towards the things that we crave, aspire to or desire. Would you ever think, "What if I earned a million dollars?" "What if I found the love of my life?" "What if I landed my dream job?" No, that phrase would likely begin more along the lines of, "How awesome would it be if...?" or "I want..." If you're a big "What if"-er I challenge you to stop letting that phrase frighten you, and start trying to have some fun with it. Every time you think up a scary "what if," thought, immediately try to replace it with some of your wildest fantasies and see what happens. At the very least, it's an interesting experiment to play with.

So imagine for a moment that your mind is plugged directly into ground zero of all that encompasses the human condition and that data is continuously flooding your brain, lighting up the emotional centers of your brain like a Christmas tree. You are not only flooded with continuous information, but you are also taking on the emotional life of said information twenty-four/seven.

People who live with anxiety and panic disorder tend to experience a rich emotional life here on earth, in some ways more so than most. But the fence swings both ways and it can be a rough ride at times. We have a tendency to laugh harder than most, love harder than most and achieve more than most in the creative fields. We also tend to cry harder, experience more pain and anxiety, and oftentimes take on emotions that simply don't belong to us. They are channeled from other outside sources even when we don't want to channel them. I've since learned that those of us who experience this are called "Empaths." Go figure. For this reason, too much negative, confusing or chaotic energy can throw us over the edge. I have become a master at monitoring the energy that surrounds me out of survival.

The tricky thing about anxiety is that it has certain landmark signs and symptoms, sure, but in some ways it is always changing its face. In this way, it is sneaky and insidious.

Just when you feel you have mastered and outsmarted its more notable physical manifestations of perspiration, heart palpitations, dizziness, confusion, feelings of unreality, and shaking *(a few examples)*, anxiety will come to you at a later time in your life disguised as a different character entirely. You may, at a later date, be caught off guard by dreadful, doomsday thoughts, phobias, night sweats or some other newly minted symptom as you are left to assume it couldn't possibly be a completely different manifestation of the same old pest: Anxiety. Like the popular Transformer action figures, anxiety can be the ultimate Transformer.

My younger years weren't all bad by any means, and my mother was a conscientious woman who made it her business to introduce me to all that New York had to offer. She was constantly taking me to Broadway musicals, museum exhibits, the Bronx Zoo, and every other landmark opportunity that living near Manhattan afforded us. She also took great pains at decorating my bedroom with beautiful pink accessories, white eyelet bedding, wallpaper *(the 1980s were big on wallpaper)* and French-inspired bedroom furniture. She loved to buy me beautiful clothing, she taught me how to blow-out my naturally curly hair into a classic Farrah Fawcett pile of soft feathery waves, and her favorite word was, and still is, "special," as in, "Oh, wow. *That's* special!" Haha. My heart swells when she says that to my son after he recounts something important he just accomplished or enjoyed.

My father, like *his* father *(my Papa Morty)*, has always been a strong, take-no- prisoners, self-made man who specializes in overcoming obstacles and fighting for what he believes in. Kindred spirits from the start, though we often butted heads throughout my childhood into my adolescents, my father raised me to continue his legacy. I'm not speaking of a conscious indoctrination, but more of a meeting of the minds that would continue to this day. My father taught me to be a fighter, a believer, and a truth-teller. These qualities that are revered in men, are oftentimes criticized in women. Such has been the dichotomy and challenge of my life thus far. It's made me a misfit, but a proud misfit.

Though both of my parents have special gifts and attributes, the tension of their whirlwind romance, their young marriage and value discrepancies caused my father to finally cry "Uncle" in 1984, when they were both thirty-four years old. My parents decided to separate when I was 9 and my little brother, David, was 4 ½.

The following year was an absurd rollercoaster ride of growing pains for both of my parents. I watched in surreal bemusement as my mother instantly dropped her leftover "baby weight," began to wear tighter fitting clothing, cut her hair into a shorter punk-rock sort of pixie cut, and made a slew of newly separated and divorced female friends. I suppose she was making lemonade from lemons. My father began to travel a lot, hit the bar scene, and indulge in alcohol and women. On one business trip to Dallas, Texas, my father, then thirty-four, hooked up with a twenty-five year old woman with whom he began an intense relationship. He soon became a regular visitor to the Dallas area. I guess you could say he was living there part time; existing off fumes of sexual chemistry, 40-proof vodka and Delta Airlines jet fuel.

As many newly single parents do, and which I now understand and don't judge as harshly, my father became very wrapped up in his newfound freedom, an exciting new romance, and contradictory feelings of guilt and displacement that I would come to know when my own relationship crumbled. He and I are kindred souls, after all; prone to the same patterns of loyalty and restlessness, pleasure-seeking and guilt.

It's interesting that as I write this, I am noticing that I judged my father less harshly than I did my mother for his post-breakup breakout, so to speak. The double standard troubles me, but my feelings are my feelings.

I can remember the pit in my stomach as my parents' divorce progressed and the almost audible guttural thud when a process server came to our front door one afternoon to serve my mother with divorce papers. "This is it," I thought. "We're now a statistic. No going back."

My brother was barely five by this point so I couldn't really talk with him about our home life, or the change in our lifestyle that occurred over that year.

We went from shopping at high-end clothing boutiques to picking through flea markets and discount stores. We counted our pennies. My funniest memory of this whole unfortunate episode was that my mother, who was not exactly a fiscal strategist, insisted on saving money in the strangest of ways. A random example: she flat out refused to buy us our brand-name Oreo cookies, instead opting for the discount store brand equivalent. What could she have saved by doing that, a dollar a week? I can remember the look and taste of those store brand Oreo knockoffs like it was yesterday. They were horrible, but my brother and I ate them because they looked like Oreos. With each bite we would imagine that they didn't taste like the bottom of our shoes. I am aware that there are families who consistently struggle much more than we ever did. But as a kid, what you don't know, you don't know. Up until that point I only knew from an upper-middle class existence. Plus, it was one more bitter pill to swallow on top of the growing chaos surrounding our home life.

Just as we were settling into our new lives as a split up family, living on a single mother's budget, my father announced that he was taking my mother, my brother and I out for dinner because we needed to discuss something important as a family. We all settled into a table at a local Italian eatery and as I tried to focus on my pasta my father blurted out, "Your mother and I are getting back together. What do you think about that?" Yes, I know it's every kid's dream who lives in a broken home that mom and dad would magically re-unite. But this reunion didn't pass the smell test with me. I could see that both my mother and father appeared happy, even elated, and dare I say back in love. But instinctually I knew there was more to this story.

In what seemed like a flash, my father had moved back into our home, he became a more engaged parent, once again, and my mother announced to me and David that she was pregnant.

New York City c.1997. Photo by Robert Milazzo.

CHAPTER FOUR

"I personally think everybody is flawed."
–told to me by Peter Facinelli

The first time I ever experienced what I would label "depression," I was eleven years old. It was late spring in 1986 and I was curled up next to my new baby brother, Jared's, crib as he rolled around and cooed. I looked at him through the bars with amazement, confusion, sadness and a feeling of loneliness that I couldn't quite articulate. The feverish pace at which everything had unfolded in my family that past year left me feeling a little cast aside. From my perspective, I felt that throughout my parents' yearlong separation they regressed from parents to two people in the throes of a second adolescents, each trying to find themselves. Once they called off their divorce I could barely settle back into a regular routine before my mother announced her pregnancy with my second brother, Jared, and things would change once again.

To clarify, I was excited to have another sibling and adored staring at the new baby in the house. I crooned ballads by Whitney Houston to him as he gazed up dreamily from his blanket on the floor. I loved playing with him. I wondered why my sense of security at home hadn't improved and I began to experience a re-visitation of physical symptoms punctuated by obsessive thoughts and ritualistic behaviors. But generally, I was just feeling sad and alone at times. Sadness is not exactly depression and depression does not necessarily translate into pure melancholy sadness. I recently heard feminist icon Gloria Steinem recite the following quote during an interview with Oprah Winfrey. I'm paraphrasing a little bit here: "When you're depressed you care about nothing. When you're sad, you care about everything."

I was somewhere in the middle.

In between the usual routine of school, Hebrew school, homework, a few close friends and spending time with my family, I would periodically be intruded upon by thoughts that seemed vaguely threatening and foreign.

Lock the door and check it three times or something bad might happen.

"Um, *excuse me*?!" The silent voice probed me and convinced me not to tempt fate, so off I went to lock the nearest door I could find, and then proceed to check that it was locked, one, two, and three times. Done. Ok.

Touch the wall as you walk by if you want to stay safe.

Once again I figured, I'll just touch the wall to be extra safe. No big deal, right?

I didn't understand where this silent voice was coming from, but as the days and weeks progressed, so did these odd requests that didn't seem to be coming from me. Now, remember I was just eleven and then twelve years old. I didn't know what OCD was. I had never even heard the term, "Obsessive Compulsive Disorder." I thought I was flat out hearing voices and going bat shit crazy.

One sunny afternoon I was in the car with my mother, and in an off-hand manner I announced that I was scared because I was "hearing voices," as I plainly put it to her.

"*WHAT*?!!" She wailed, as she pulled over and screeched the car to a screaming halt. I could see in her eyes that my mother was genuinely worried and ready to hightail it to the nearest psychiatrist.

That was when it occurred to me that maybe I hadn't phrased my problem properly. Let me just state that I am in no way trivializing or making light of mental illnesses such as Schizophrenia or Bi-polar Disorder. I am simply explaining how my OCD was interpreted by me as a pre-teen who wasn't able to accurately understand or articulate what I was experiencing.

I then proceeded to explain that for quite some time I had been hearing silent, in-audible voices which were essentially obsessive thoughts that were urging me to engage in compulsive rituals to keep any anxiety or depressive feelings at bay. In other words, my unconscious mind had developed the beginnings of an unhealthy coping mechanism to dump my anxiety and depression into.

I began to seek out solace at the local video store across from my school. I checked out VHS tapes like vintage *Saturday Night Live* episodes and stand-up comedy by the likes of Eddie Murphy, Richard Pryor and Robin Williams. I tried to laugh my way to a happier place and sometimes I would even re-play some of the funnier moments from those videos like a loop in my head to crowd out the thoughts that haunted me. Call it self-medicating with comedy? Hey, there are worse ways to self-medicate and I stayed far away from those!

Apart from great comedy, my OCD was still a virtual landfill for all of my unwanted feelings of anxiety. And my depression was a catch-all for the shame and embarrassment I felt for not being able to adequately control it. As my OCD grew stronger and more sophisticated in its methods of shoving my anxiety into the recesses of my unconscious mind, there was naturally some overflow. For the most part I learned to function normally with this emotional monkey on my back, but sometimes things would reach critical mass and I would experience a panic attack.

By this point I felt safe telling my parents about the panic attacks, particularly my mother who has also suffered from a panic disorder throughout her life. She became my security blanket and my lifeline. But as a middle school and eventually high school-age kid, I wanted to go out to the movies or to dinner with friends on a Friday or Saturday night to blow off some steam. I couldn't always be near those nearest and dearest to me; I couldn't always be in my comfort zone, and at that time there were no cellphones *(the anxiety sufferers' handheld courage)*. I was relegated to searching for a pay phone should a crisis arise, and when it came to my anxiety and panic, I was still a novice. I didn't understand anything about my own body or my own mind, let alone how to navigate these dark waters.

I can recall being in a movie theatre at around the age of fifteen or sixteen years old and experiencing feelings of unreality, detachment, dizziness, heart palpitations, blurry vision, a lump in my throat and a looming sense of doom. After suffering in silence for the better part of an hour, I burst out of my seat in the movie theatre, my friend *(also named Alison, but with one L)* trailing behind me as I made a beeline for the payphone in the Syosset, Long Island movie theatre lobby.

I phoned my house and told my mother I was in a fit of terror and had to be picked up from the movie theatre at once, and taken home. As I was crying and describing my physical symptoms to my mother, she tried to calm me with deep breathing techniques and the reassurance that all of the physical sensations shooting through my petrified body were anxiety and nothing more. From what I remember, she managed to talk me off the ledge. But when I hung up the phone and turned to my friend, she had a look of horror on her face and I felt judged and defective. I felt humiliated, and to this day she still brings up that episode at the movies in 1991. It's not with malice. But she might say something like, "I remember how you had so much anxiety when we were young. Do you remember when you had to call your mom from the movies in high school? You really scared me that night."

Thanks.

During my high school existence it was not lost on my parents that mainstream academics were not exactly my forte. I often spent more time cutting out of school than sitting in class. The way I saw it, I had better things to do with my time than to sit through mathematics, earth science or some teacher's slanted propagandized version of our country's history. I was into the arts and I loved to read movie scripts, plays and biographies in the school library. Sometimes I would visit a friend during their art or music class or simply leave the school's campus and grab a bite to eat. In short, I did what I wanted. I have always had an independent mind and an incurable courage that didn't mesh with my anxiety-self. It's a dichotomous bag of qualities. I could always fearlessly tell the truth, stand up for what I believe in no matter the consequences or embark on a seemingly impossible path that would make most people recoil in fear. Public speaking is a piece of cake for me, and I'll communicate my feelings to another without flinching.

So why the white knuckling in some of the most seemingly innocuous of situations? What is important to understand, whether you are simply reading about me or relating this to yourself, is that some of the strongest, most intelligent and creative human beings throughout history have lived with various degrees of anxiety disorder. I consider myself a person of rarefied strength. At times, when I've been inclined to beat myself up, I have to remind myself of it.

If you're reading this book and I sound like you, please note: you are stronger than you think, and you are stronger in ways where others lack your unique brand of courage. People with anxiety are courageous every time we feel anxious and forge ahead despite our discomfort.

Driving on the highway *(a biggie for my mom!)*, flying in a plane, making a speech, socializing at a crowded party, waiting on test results, trying to measure up in front of your boss at work… whatever your anxiety triggers are, you should pat yourself on the back every time you thumb your nose at the fear and walk through it to get it done.

As my high school days wore on I noticed that non-fiction biographical books lured me more and more. I would often spend my lunch period sitting at a table in the school library, reading about various public figures. I was fascinated by their childhoods, their coming-of-age, their mistakes, and their journey of redemption and ultimate success. Sounds like a nerdy pastime, I know, but I found it incredibly therapeutic. Just as that very first time I picked up a biography on Madonna and started pouring through it, I never tired of searching for clues in every book that revealed the humanity behind a public figure; something I could hold on to and relate to myself.

It would also eventually be the initial catalyst that would spark my career as a journalist, though I didn't put two and two together at this time in my life.

CHAPTER FIVE

"My entire career has been based upon not just being a sex star. It's about being a well-rounded star, not just being good at sex."
–told to me by Jenna Jameson

Just her name elicits thoughts of salacious, juicy tidbits. Wouldn't you agree? I bet you're thinking, "Oooh… this chapter is going to be good!" Jenna Jameson was a figure who intrigued me for quite some time. And ok, I will admit that I have always been drawn to the adult entertainment world in some strange, obscure, voyeuristic way.

You might be thinking, "Yeah, you and everyone else. That's why we watch it." But that's not really what I mean. Here's something I have never, and I mean *never*, admitted out in the open until right this very second. Here goes: had my life unfolded differently, I can easily see myself having become a porn star. Let me explain…

Growing up I felt like something of an ugly duckling, mainly because I was an exceptionally late bloomer. I was often ridiculed by a few obnoxious male classmates for my then underdeveloped chest and being rather short and skinny throughout my middle school and early high school years. I think I also felt that way inside, as my self-esteem was surely a work in progress. Emotionally speaking, I was under construction for so many years, much like that one road in your hometown that seems to be getting worked on indefinitely, with no completion in sight. You just see a construction crew, trucks, and random cones for years, and wonder what they're doing with our tax dollars.

As high school rolled on into college I had resigned myself to being the adorable, scrappy tomboy. Why did I need to bother with girly things anyway? My father had raised me to learn how to fight, to be street smart and to talk like a truck driver on steroids if you got in my face in a way I didn't like. I was kind of cute, but I was the tough girl known more for my left hook than my banging body. In the early nineties I figured it was all about flannel button downs, baggy jeans and high top Timbs. And of course a beeper affixed to my front jeans pocket.

Suddenly something shifted and I began to yearn for male attention. I felt this raw, unbridled sensuality start to spring to life inside of me just as I was turning twenty-one. I began to blossom fast and furiously one summer as I took notice of the fact that under all of that flannel and denim I was beginning to develop quite the delicious hourglass figure. My hair had grown long and lush, and my face matured and all of my features suddenly fit perfectly into place, punctuated by flattering cheekbones. You might think I have a detached feeling about my looks as if I was some dude describing a girl he has the hots for. But I've always viewed my physicality as nothing more than a costume, an avatar. I recognize my true self as my soul; the person writing this book; the observer of it all.

I suddenly became all about my looks, my sensuality and sexuality, and male attention became the fuel in my tank. Couple that with a tumultuous relationship with my father that left me strung out with teenage angst and rebellion, and I was ready to act out. And here's the kicker, I had no idea who I really was on the inside. My whole existence became about external approval, attention and validation, and yes, that is dangerous. I had no understanding of my own intelligence, talents, spiritual center. I was like a stealth Kamikaze pilot going 600 miles per hour into a gloriously spectacular nosedive.

When, at twenty-three years of age, I packed up all of my belongings and moved to Los Angeles, California, my relationship with my father was worse than ever. We clashed constantly like oil and water, and our fights left me scarred and broken inside, in ways I couldn't even understand at the time. I feel that he was struggling in the same way. We loved each other, but we were both hurting as a result of the state of our father-daughter relationship.

I had just shot a two page spread for Playboy, for their 1998 annual *Playboy's College Girls* issue. The pictorial featured one full page of a full frontal nude image of me on the left side page, and on the opposite page was a 5 picture collage of me wearing a corset-style shirt, a barely-there white thong and black lace-up boots in various stages of undress; in a library setting of all places. It made me feel validated when I learned that thousands of girls all over the country had competed to make it into that particular issue. I liked that feeling. I liked being naked, being thought of as sexy, and I wanted more. When I went out on dates, I would transform my naturally tomboyish style sensibility into a bombshell image with glamorous makeup, big flowing hair and skimpy outfits that showed off my then-perfect proportions. In fact, one time I donned a mini-skirt and left the underwear at home. That outfit was punctuated by knee-high iridescent platform boots, and to answer your burning question: my date and I wound up in a two year relationship. No, it had nothing to do with the boots but they didn't hurt. He was actually one of the first people to try to make me see the beauty I held inside that I was just too closed off and stubborn to see for myself.

Playboy was not a glamorous, flawless experience for me. I had been modeling for various photographers around New York City to earn some extra cash while in college. One particular shot of me donning a flesh colored bikini with my eyes closed was made into a promotional poster for a glamour modeling convention taking place in New Jersey. I was asked to be there to take pictures with people and just kind of walk around. Frankly, I didn't really know what I was doing there. The event was filled to the brim with Playboy Playmates who were there to sell autographed magazines and other memorabilia. I was bored and struck up a conversation with a model named Lynn Thomas, who was fresh off her reign as Playmate of the Month, Miss May 1997. Though I looked younger and less sophisticated than my twenty-two years, and didn't exactly boast Playmate proportioned assets at that time, Lynn mentioned to me that she thought I had the perfect look for Playboy's Newsstand Special issues. She told me she thought the production director of those issues, a woman named Debbie May, would go nuts for my brunette girl-next-door looks. She asked me to send her some of my modeling shots and said that she would pass them along for me. So the next day without missing a beat, I dropped some photographs in the mail for Lynn to look through.

Lynn Thomas passed my photos along on a Friday and that Monday I got a call from a bouncy young woman with a cheery hi-pitched voice. It was Debbie May. She introduced herself on the phone telling me, "Your pictures are adorable. I need you to come to my studio to test with my photographer, Gen." I took the address down, thanked her, and showed up on the appointed day only to find myself surrounded by about fifty other girls who were also there to test for a spot in an upcoming issue. I was a nervous wreck, and desperately wanted to leave. I instantly questioned my decision to pursue this and as I sat in a holding area with other young would-be models who had no interest in being warm or friendly towards me *(their competition)*, my anxiety only grew. Gen, the photographer, sauntered into the holding area, proclaiming, "Ok, which beautiful, brave girl is next up to shoot?" I panicked and sprung up from my seat, ready to bolt the hell out of there, when I felt a hand on my shoulder firmly spinning me around. It was Gen. He smiled and led me over to the studio part of the loft. I didn't know what to do, so I simply followed his lead.

All of us girls were instructed to bring with us a bikini swimsuit and a pair of high heels for the test shoot. Gen instructed me to put on my bikini bottoms and my high heeled shoes only, no top, and to stand still until he instructed me how to pose for the test shots. I acquiesced and as soon as I was topless began to hyper ventilate. There I was in skimpy bikini bottoms, sky high pumps, boobs freely sprung and I couldn't catch my breath. Good God! I was indeed having a panic attack! Only me. Looking back, I have to laugh at myself. I felt so stupid like I'd wasted everyone's time, but Gen put down his camera, walked over to me and said, "*Breathe.* You're going to do great." Suddenly I thought, "I *am* going to do great," and I began posing like I was born to pose semi-nude for the camera. I was finding my angles, gently swinging my hair, raising my right eyebrow, giving three-quarter angles to the camera. I tried my best to channel every famous Playboy model I'd ever seen in the magazine issues at my cousin's house from when I was in high school.

The test shoot ended as quickly as it began and Gen went running over to Debbie May's desk, freshly dried Polaroids swinging in his grip. Debbie motioned me over and said she needed to book me for an upcoming issue right away. I was flattered at their sense of urgency and as she was talking details I zoned out and pictured myself posing in the most glamorous, sexy lingerie for their *Playboy's Book of Lingerie* issue. When I came to, I heard her make mention of *Playboy's College Girls*. "Oh, sorry. I thought this would be for *Book of Lingerie*." She kind of looked me up and down and then said, "Oh, well you can do that one eventually too, but I have to have you in our annual *College Girls* issue." I had one foot out the door at the CW Post Campus of Long Island University where I had been attending school. I was still there for one last semester on a technicality, because I had failed to complete one elective class in computers which I needed in order to earn my Bachelor's Degree.

As my twenties edged towards thirty, I was beginning to come into my own, with a public relations career and the very beginnings of what would blossom into my journalism career, interviewing public figures. I was moving in the right direction by all outward accounts, but I was still full of rebellious venom and I hadn't yet found a productive way to channel it.

A friend of mine who was a talent manager told me about a new television show that was being produced for Cinemax's late night line-up. When I was younger, I can remember jokingly referring to that type of content as "Skinemax," because of the gratuitous love scenes and nudity. When he mentioned the casting process to me, I told him that I wanted to attend and audition, to which he glanced at me sideways. By that point I was operating my own boutique PR firm and starting to write articles for the website PR.com. You read that right. If there is one thing I know for sure it is this: spiritual sickness has an unexcelled ability to override intelligence.

I booked that job for Cinemax, and accepted. That's when my conscience began doing gymnastics in my mind. My off and on again boyfriend at the time promptly scolded me and warned me that I would soon live to regret my immature decision. My manager friend told me to dump my boyfriend *(obvious opposing agendas)*. I then called a high school friend of mine who happens to be a well-known sex educator and "*sexpert*" in the adult field. She proceeded to support what I was embarking on. Finally, I called an ex-boyfriend who said something to me that really resonated and I still think about it to this day. He said, "Sometimes you have to knock up against your boundaries to discover what they are." "Brilliant!" I thought. And I decided to go through with the television series. Of course I continued to flip flop a little in my head. I certainly had a case of cold feet on the morning of the shoot as my car made its way up a steep winding road in the San Fernando Valley, towards the hilltop mansion that the production had rented for the day's shoot. But I had agreed to perform the role, and there was money on the line for the production company and for Cinemax. I did not want to flake out on an entire set of people who were there to work for the day. I had to go through with it.

In the meantime, I began to become very much entrenched in my blossoming career as a fledgling journalist. I was slowly but surely booking interviews with people like Joy Behar, Leeza Gibbons, and Katrina Campins, from the very first season of *The Apprentice*. I recently drove up the California coast to Malibu to interview and profile the editorial team of Malibu Magazine. One of my favorite interviews from that very early time period was with a woman named Dina LaPolt. Dina was and still is the attorney for the estate and posthumous career of the late rapper, Tupac Shakur. She worked in partnership with Tupac's mother, the late Afeni Shakur. Together, Dina and Afeni worked to untangle all of Tupac's assets, music royalties, and such, after his passing. This dynamic duo coagulated, preserved, developed and managed Tupac's entire brand as a continued global bestselling artist. She was instrumental in assisting Afeni Shakur in creating the Tupac Amaru Shakur Foundation (TASF) and The Tupac Amaru Shakur Center for the Arts in Stone Mountain, Georgia. In addition, Dina was one of the producer's on the documentary film about Tupac's life, *Tupac: Resurrection*, which was nominated for an Oscar in 2005 for Best Documentary Feature Film. Through all of this, I discovered that I was finding my voice; I was finding a powerful yet productive and positive outlet for my anger, my joy, my love, my talent and my need to express my myself. As my roster of interviewees grew, and my writing and production quality improved, so did my self-esteem. Discovering that I was a writer and forging a path as a self-taught and self-made journalist saved my life.

I no longer felt the need to be an exhibitionist, to flaunt my sexuality or to put myself in any sort of compromising positions. I was now thirty years old and finally I knew who I was. And, as if synchronized, my relationship with my family, particularly my father, began to rapidly improve.

I still hold a fascination with various subcultures and alternative lifestyles because on some level I can relate. I understand what it is to be injured emotionally and spiritually. I understand having an overwhelming need to express oneself, to be seen, to be loved and admired, and how that intention can misfire without the right tools at one's disposal. The older I get, the more my judgment erodes and gives way to compassion and curiosity.

Yes, I was very anxious to nab the opportunity for a sit down with Jenna Jameson…

At the time it was 2007, and Jenna was at a professional peek, both in traditional mainstream media and in emerging social media like MySpace. People stood in awe of this woman who had the chutzpa to dare to cross over from adult entertainment into mainstream celebrity status, who had the vision to brand herself in a way that no other adult performer ever had, and the audacity to create her own production and distribution company, Club Jenna. Her memoir, *How to Make Love Like a Porn Star* was a huge bestseller and she seemed to be on top of the world, yet incredibly vulnerable.

After a little detective work, I managed to track down the public relations firm that handled Jenna's company, Club Jenna. I put in a detailed interview request which was then passed around to her personal team. Shortly thereafter, I received a group email between the Club Jenna corporate PR firm, Jenna Massoli *(Jameson's birth and legal name)*, an executive assistant to Jenna named Linda Johnson, and some other relevant team members. They all seemed pretty excited to set this up, which I loved!

I was falling more and more in love with journalism as both a job and an art form. I couldn't wait to pick this woman's brain, to really get inside and find out what made her tick in a way that no other journalist had ever done.

Shortly before my interview with Jenna was scheduled to take place, an issue of US Weekly hit the newsstands with Jenna Jameson on the cover. She had given them an exclusive about her recent brush with skin cancer; Melanoma to be exact. I was utterly deflated, thinking, "How the hell am I supposed to follow *that* act?! An exclusive about Melanoma? Just great!" For a minute, I thought my goal of producing the best Jenna Jameson interview ever was dead in the water, until…

It was presidential primary season in the spring of 2007 with Barack Obama, Hillary Clinton and John Edwards vying for the Democratic nomination, and at that time it was still anyone's race. Candidates were looking to pick up funding, endorsements and clout to pad their campaigns.

I researched Jenna's life thoroughly, reading her book from cover-to-cover, learning about her days as a contract girl with Wicked Pictures and the development of her own company, Club Jenna. I watched her *E! True Hollywood Story*, spoke with people in the know about her life, and yes, watched some of her movies. I sat down to write out my questions and I wasn't pulling any punches; I wanted to know all.

I wrote out questions about her adolescence, the past sexual assaults she'd suffered, her late mother, her desire for children *(she hadn't yet had her twin boys)*, her experiences in shooting porn, what she gets asked by both men and women, her views on feminism, how she views her reputation; I mean, I asked it all. As I was wrapping up my list of questions on the page I decided to write questions asking Jenna her thoughts on how politics has impacted pornography, both during the Clinton administration, and into the George W. Bush years. I rounded out this line of questioning by jotting down a note to myself to ask Jenna which candidate struck her fancy for the upcoming 2007/2008 presidential election cycle.

On the day of the interview I glanced over my questions, and seeing how extensive and probing they were, I felt a bit nervous. I hoped they would be taken in good spirits. I said my silent prayer that I now said before every interview, asking that my questions be received by my interview subject in the spirit in which they were asked. I then placed a call to Linda Johnson to confirm the timing and go over some ground rules regarding Jenna.

At the time, Jenna had gone through a taxing divorce from her ex-husband and business partner, Jay Grdena, and she had lost what appeared to be an alarming amount of weight. The only thing Linda asked was that I focus my questioning away from Jenna's weight and around more substantial topics, to which I agreed. I had much more interesting stuff up my sleeve, anyway. Linda then said, "You're going to love Jenna, she's the best! She'll talk your ear off."

On the afternoon of our scheduled interview, the originally scheduled interview time of 1 PM EST came and went, and no sign of Jenna. Finally at around 1:30 or so the phone rang. "Hi baby, it's Jenna. I'm so sorry but I'm at the dentist and running a bit late. I will call you a soon as I get home." We agreed to reconvene at around two. At 2 PM Jenna called me again and said she had just arrived home from her dental appointment and she was in pain from her procedure. When she asked if I'd like to talk right then or once she had a chance to settle in and make herself more comfortable, I chose the latter.

Here's something that I have always secretly loved, and this is a bit embarrassing to admit. I actually loved it when the celebrity I was scheduled to interview either was late for our meeting or had some other sort of hiccup in our mutually planned schedule. It actually made me less nervous and I felt that I had the upper hand because the conversation usually started off with them apologizing for running late. It had a tendency to break the ice and they were more eager to please and redeem themselves during the interview.

Upon finally sitting down to speak with Jenna she was instantly familiar with me and we had a great rapport. There were no awkward moments, as casual conversation bled into the formality of our interview. During our ninety minute conversation, I asked and she told. Nothing was off limits. Even as I asked her if wanting for her long-deceased mother since early childhood, and being raped multiple times, coaxed her towards the adult industry, she was forthcoming and candid with me. We talked about graphic sexuality, but we also talked about typical girl things like love and relationships, and how *(at the time)* she was excited at the prospect of having children and giving them a better childhood than she had. We discussed feminism, her business acumen, male and female double standards, and she delighted in the fact that my conservative mother knew who she was.

We had a good laugh when I asked her if it feels weird and anxiety-provoking to walk down the street knowing that half of the free world has watched her have sex. She responded with humor, stating, "Absolutely! I mean, I think that you would have to be an alien not to have those kinds of feelings. Every once in a while I'll be sitting with my boyfriend and a guy will come up to me and say, "Oh my God! I j*****off to you so many times in college!" And I'm just like, "What do I say to that?!" "LOL" wasn't a thing back then or the interview transcript would have been riddled with it. There was a lot of LOLing going on.

With many celebrities, I kind of had to play make believe with them and do this dance where I tried my best to skirt around the nitty gritty of an issue. It's either because their publicist insists upon it, or simply because I want to save the other person and myself the embarrassment of blatantly pointing out the pink polka dotted elephant in the room.

In the case with Jenna, her attitude was, "Bring it. I can handle it." She wasn't in denial about who and what she is, and how she is perceived.

Here's how the rest of that particular line of questioning unfolded:

Jenna Jameson: … So the people who date me have to be very, very secure. Every once in a while I get a little bit weirded out, because I feel like I'm kind of a normal girl, and I get embarrassed by the same things. I'm shy when it comes to that stuff. Especially if my friends are like, "Oh, I was switching through the channels and I rolled over the Jenna channel…" because I have my own channel, and they're like, "Oh my God! I saw you having sex and it totally freaked me out!!" That to me is the most embarrassing, when my friends see me naked or see me in movies. Strangers, I can handle.

Allison Kugel: Do your friends generally avoid it?

Jenna Jameson: Oh my God, yes! They cannot even look at me that way. They know me as Jenna Massoli, not Jenna Jameson. They know the dorky, silly girl. Jenna Jameson is a character. If I were Jenna Jameson 100% of the time, I would be really sore (laughs).

Allison Kugel: (Laughs) Well, you only do a few movies a year, right?

Jenna Jameson: At the height of my career, we released two [movies] a year. I seriously have had less mileage than most women. But I don't really talk about that, because people want to think that I am this monster, and complete sexual freak. I can't really deny that, because in bed I am crazy and I love sex. I have sex two, three times a day with my boyfriend. [But] if I don't have a boyfriend, or if I'm not married, or whatever, I don't have sex. It's not like I can just go out and meet a guy and have sex with him. It just doesn't work like that for me. First of all, I am so incredibly intimidating to men. I couldn't get laid if I wanted to. That probably sounds weird, but, I scare the living pants off men.

Throughout the entire interview I kept waiting for that "gotcha" moment when I would surely be able to detect something off-balance about her. I can honestly say, I never did. In fact, what I was presented with was someone who was much more intelligent than many of the so-called normal people I regularly socialize with, yet there is a duality to her. At the time, still entrenched in the adult movie business, Jenna was forced to be half porn star/half girl-next-door, and she learned how to live that dichotomy on a daily basis.

We got caught up in the authentic flow of chit chat and I nearly forgot to include this little ditty:

Allison Kugel: Do you find that the climate of the adult industry changes when there is a Republican administration versus Democratic?

Jenna Jameson: Absolutely. The Clinton administration was the best years for the adult industry and I wish that Clinton would run again. I would love to have him back in office. I would love to have Al Gore in office. When Republicans are in office, the problem is, a lot of times they try to put their crosshairs on the adult industry, to make a point. It's sad, when there are so many different things that are going on in the world: war, and people are dying of genocide. It's sad that they feel that they have to target the sex industry, and not target the problems with insurance and the homeless and the AIDS epidemic. There are so many things that need to be cleared up before fucking pornography. I look forward to another democrat being in office. It just makes the climate so much better for us, and I know that once all our troops come home, things are going to be better and I think that getting Bush out of office is the most important thing right now.

> **Allison Kugel: Who's your favorite democratic front runner for 2008? Barack Obama, Hillary Clinton or John Edwards?**

> Jenna Jameson: I love Hillary. I think that in some ways she's pretty conservative for a democrat, but I would love to have a woman in office. I think that it would be a step in the right direction for our country, and there would be less focus on war and more focus on bettering society.

That last question wrapped up our official interview, which soon afterwards became the political endorsement heard around the world. In May of 2007, we had not yet made many of our connections in the news syndication market, so for the most part, our celebrity interview content made the rounds of online media outlets on a wing and a prayer. I would cherry pick from what I felt were the most enticing quotes from an interview and send out a few emails to bloggers and some magazine editors in hopes of generating publicity for our interviews. With the Jenna interview, I had been juggling quite a bit of work on the day when we posted her piece, so an aggressive marketing campaign for the article fell by the wayside; or so we thought.

The article was posted, and then I had to rush into the city for a gaggle of meetings. Jenna Jameson was the very last thing on my mind, until that is, I received a phone call from my editor Jason. He informed me that the blog, JustHillary.com, dedicated to covering Hillary Clinton's 2007/8 primary presidential campaign, had picked up our story, and DrudgeReport.com picked up on the JustHillary.com article which was chock full of Jenna's PR.com quotes about Hillary Clinton. Once it hit Drudge, the story caught fire and was being talked about by everyone from Rush Limbaugh and Fox News to Tucker Carlson on MSNBC, and network affiliate news programs all over the country. It was the big pop culture political story of the day, "Porn Star Jenna Jameson Endorses Hillary Clinton for President." I mean, come on. Ya gotta love it! Talk about a classic moment in time. And I'm sure Hillary and her camp were just thrilled to pieces over this one.

Before I knew it, I was reading comments about me, an unknown fledgling online journalist. Someone even wrote something to the effect of, "Perhaps interviewer Allison Kugel should stay out of the endorsement business…" I fucking loved it! I mean, I really ate it up. I, my editor Jason, my then-boyfriend Patrick, our editorial crew at PR.com, we all had a great laugh over it. Then the late night shows came on…

Oh my fucking G-d! Jay Leno, Conan O'Brien and *Saturday Night Live* were all using my interview with Jenna Jameson as late night material. Me. I had the big national scoop of the day. Patrick and I settled into bed after a long and busy day for both of us, and for some inexplicable reason we decided to watch *The Tonight Show*. I never watched *The Tonight*

Show. Jay Leno is doing his monologue, and BOOM! Here it comes. "Did you hear about Hillary Clinton's latest endorsement? Porn star Jenna Jameson has endorsed Hillary for President. I guess Bill's been calling in those favors." The television audience roared from the shock and awe at the combination of famous names rolled into one joke. Pat and I looked at each other. "That's *my* story. That's my interview with Jenna. It made *The Tonight Show*. Did that really just happen?" Later on that night I got a call from Jason. "Conan O'Brien was talking about your interview with Jenna!" Saturday rolled around and a friend of mine emailed me to say, The "Jenna Jameson endorses Hillary Clinton" story was on Weekend Update on *SNL*." I watched all of the TV clips, read all of the blog blurbs, listened to the radio clips. And then pondered how I would attempt to make lightning strike like this on a regular basis.

We were gobsmacked. I realized just how easy it is to create a national headline no matter who you are. It's a matter of ingenuity, and it's what separates great journalists from mediocre ones. That was my first real lesson in how the media worked. My next lesson would be in making sure I received my due credit for a story and leveraging it in my career. My secret became this – while everyone else was looking for the obvious money shot, I would find that jewel of a comment on a subject that the others weren't clever enough to unearth.

Another gem of a journalism truth I discovered – you don't get people to open up by drilling them with probing and invasive questions. You get people to open up by opening up, *yourself*. It disarms people and their humanity emerges.

I haven't spoken to Jenna Jameson in years, and from what I had observed in the press and heard from mutual acquaintances, she was once again struggling with addiction. To hear this was a big departure from the woman whose company I enjoyed back in 2007, and I know that having children and creating a family of her own was her biggest dream in life. I recently saw her Instagram feed where she has openly admitted to struggling with substance abuse and has now taken a strict vow of sobriety. I am proud of her.

When she is on top of her game, Jenna Jameson is a woman of fierce intelligence, humor and heart. I wish her well.

Vampir**ess**. Los Angeles, CA c. 2005. Photo by Ralph
Lliteras.

CHAPTER SIX

*"I guess most artists are misinterpreted. You
don't know what they're thinking."*
- told to me by Curtis "50 Cent" Jackson

As time progressed in my post as Senior Editor of
PR.com, celebrity interviews came to me in various
ways. There are several ways in which I booked
interviews with actors, musicians, politicians, models,
athletes… you get the picture. Sometimes I chased
after an interview; sometimes it fell into my lap.
Sometimes I requested an interview and got what I
called a swap-out. A swap-out *(my own personal lingo)*
is when you asked a publicist to interview a particular
client of theirs and instead of turning you down flat,
they counter-pitched you with another client on their
roster. Sometimes the person they counter-pitched
me with was not appropriate at all, but sometimes it
was a helluva score, at least in my opinion. Like when I
tried for, I-don't-even-remember-who, and wound up
interviewing *Glee*'s Chris Colfer instead. But almost
all of my interviews began with me scrolling through
the latest entertainment and popular culture news
stories and upcoming projects online as a matter

of daily routine. Everything from Google News and Moviefone.com to album metrics, book publisher websites, and the press release newswires. And of course, sometimes I didn't have to look further than my own email inbox, as I was pitched by publicists.

I was scrolling through PR Newswire one morning when I saw a press release put out by Interscope Records announcing the upcoming release of 50 Cent's album, *Before I Self-Destruct*. I've always been drawn to urban culture and I could probably qualify as a 1990s hip hop historian, particularly as it pertains to the late great rapper, Tupac Shakur. I'd been really into artists like Eminem and 50 Cent in the early 2000s, but in the case of Fifty, I'd only ever really listened to his more commercial, radio-friendly music.

As Senior Editor in charge of steering our ship of editorial content, I really strived for broad appeal and balance with our interviews. I wanted to reach a wide scope of readers from many different demographics, but I'll admit that I was always looking for any opportunity to bring more hip hop flavor to our content. I knew that Fifty would be a major score for us, so I sent a formal interview request over to his publicist, Yvette Gayle, at Interscope Records.

Soon enough I got a reply from Yvette asking me if I'd like to come to the offices of G-Unit Records to meet with Fifty. I accepted the invitation, and immediately picked up the phone and called my younger brother, Jared.

"Jared, I need you to come with me into the city to meet with 50 Cent at his office. You come with me and just pretend to be my assistant, ok?"

I didn't have to twist his arm. He was on board to take a car service with me into the city to meet 50 Cent. So sweet, always willing to sacrifice to help out his big sister. To this day, I'm not sure why I needed my brother to be my wingman for this interview. I don't know if I was afraid of being hit on, or if I was just plain nervous about doing the interview and needed moral support and a few laughs on the way into the city. Either way, Jared and I had fun on the ride in, as we always do when we hang out together.

I was dressed pretty conservatively in tailored pants and a formfitting emerald green sweater that came all the way up to my collarbone. I applied my natural, fresh faced makeup look which I call my "standard look," of earth tone eyeliner and shadow, a tiny bit of neutral blush on the balls of my cheeks and a neutral lip-toned gloss. I was oh-so into Angelina Jolie's ultra-understated, regal look at the time. When we arrived at the G-Unit offices, Jared and I were brought to a waiting room and offered bottles of Vitamin Water by a friendly assistant. It was just us in there until another journalist finally wondered in to gather her belongings before heading out the door. As we waited for about 30 minutes I could feel that adrenaline tension building in me that I am usually pretty good at keeping at bay until *after* an interview.

Eventually 50 Cent's publicist, Yvette, came into the waiting room and told me to follow her out onto the balcony where Fifty would be meeting with me. I was in a little bit of a fog, just trying to focus on the task at hand. Before I knew it my brother had tailed us and plopped himself down on a chair out on the balcony before I could say, "What are you doing? Go wait outside in the waiting area." Fifty then walked out to greet me *(us)*. He was friendly and open from the start, giving me a hug and kiss on the cheek, and sitting beside me at a small bistro-style table and chairs out on the balcony. My brother perched at another identical bistro table set that was also on the large balcony. Jared got awfully comfortable, stretching out and typing away on his laptop computer like it was any other work day.

Here's an excerpt from the opening paragraph of my originally published interview with 50 Cent. It illustrates our rapport when we first sat down together:

> "The first thing I said to him after he greeted me with a warm hug was, 'Should I call you Curtis?' to which he quietly replied, 'That's fine,' as he looked down at his hands for a beat and then back up at me with a sheepish smile spreading across his face. At that moment what rushed through my mind was the fleeting thought, 'Is

> it my imagination, or am I making this guy a
> bit nervous?' In that instant my own butterflies
> were settled. That initial blind date atmosphere
> that interviews can often resemble had instantly
> dissipated."

I remember this interview like it was yesterday.
I think it's because I am a very sensory-oriented
person and there was a lot in the atmosphere
to take in, and commit to my hyperactive sense-
memory. The balcony off the G-Unit offices was
catty-cornered and the view was breathtaking in
both directions. You could hear the muffled roar
of the traffic down below. Fifty was dressed in a
black baseball cap, worn-in black leather jacket
and plain cotton T-shirt. Nothing fancy; no jewelry,
nothing that would scream, or even whisper, his
then net worth. His best accessories are his eyes
and smile, they dance in a childlike way.

As we were settling in I remembered that we did
have some common frames of reference. Our
sons have similar names, and he and my mother
attended the same Queens, New York high school,
Andrew Jackson. We were talking about his
difficulty having to grow up without his mom and
the financial burden it placed on his hardworking
grandparents. We talked about the challenges of
raising our sons, which led to this ice-breaking
exchange:

> **Allison Kugel: By the way, my son's name is Marcus.**

> 50 Cent (Curtis Jackson): My son's name is Marquise!

> **Allison Kugel: Yes, I know. Funny. And my mother actually went to your high school, Andrew Jackson. But she's a sixty year old Jewish woman.**

> 50 Cent (Curtis Jackson): *(Laughs).*

What made this interview comical to me was that Fifty and I engaged in some good-natured heated debate about rap music and its message towards, and about, women. Every time he was losing the argument he would nudge my brother in the arm or ribs to bring him into the fold and gain an ally for the male side of the debate. My brother would just laugh, shrug or throw out a non-committal word or two, and go right back to whatever he was supposedly doing on his laptop.

I was unintimidated and undeterred by Fifty's attempt at outnumbering me with his men against woman strategy. Here's an excerpt from some of our verbal sparring:

> **Allison Kugel: I have to ask you, what is your general opinion of women? The impression**

you give from a distance is that it's not good. You're a sweetheart, but from what people see in the media it doesn't seem like you think very highly of women, generally speaking.

50 Cent (Curtis Jackson): That's not true. What they misinterpret is, when you choose to write the harsh realities, you write [about] different classes. If I took you downstairs there's a store that says "For Adults," and me and you are both adults, right?

Allison Kugel: Yes, I passed that store.

50 Cent (Curtis Jackson): That store has entertainment in it. Now check this out ... the women that we were just talking about, it isn't the same women that you were making reference to. What I'm trying to say to you is that, that is a different class of woman that's in that adult entertainment space.

Allison Kugel: The women who are in those movies...

50 Cent (Curtis Jackson): Right. So they're on that tape and they get paid a thousand dollars to perform whatever you would feel is intimate.

Allison Kugel: To have sex...

50 Cent (Curtis Jackson): Right, in every way possible! And guess what? You're gonna find every kind of shape and from a woman's perspective you could point and find every kind of woman that you think physically meets the description of attractive. You could look and say, "She looks nice." From a female perspective, you will find a representation of beauty in every creed. We find African-American women, white women, Brazilian women, Hawaiian women. There's actually categories. You could just go and ask for it. Whatever you want, you could find it. You know what these women are representation of? These women are representation of whores. They fuck for a thousand dollars with no royalties, in the film that you're watching.

Allison Kugel: What about the guy who's in the film who is making even less money?

50 Cent (Curtis Jackson): Them too. But socially it's something different from a male perspective, the lust factor that [men have] for women. Women are beautiful. They're better than men to look at. So there would probably be a clear statement to say that men lust after women more than women lust for men.

Allison Kugel: Those are the women you're talking about when you're rapping about women?

50 Cent (Curtis Jackson): You're making representation to a different class of woman at different points on the record. The average woman doesn't make the separation. She either hears something that she thinks is disrespectful, or she doesn't know that it wasn't for her. A lot of times the women that do enjoy the art form are no longer sensitive to those statements or things being said in that manner, because they feel like that doesn't apply to them, and they do acknowledge that those women are out there. If you hear a derogatory statement within the music, that artist is probably making reference to something he's experienced that made him feel like that woman was that kind of woman.

Allison Kugel: In my adolescence I remember being angry because my father was a strong influence on me growing up, and I grew up around my brothers and male cousins and I wanted to be like them. When I heard [lyrics] like that I felt like it was saying I can't be like them because I'm a second class citizen as a woman.

50 Cent (Curtis Jackson): What?! Second class citizen?! There's standards from a male perspective that are different from women. Your brother, if he sleeps with four women in a ten or twelve block radius while he's a single male there's absolutely nothing wrong with that. If you applied the same standards to you,

within the neighborhood you would have an aura of a whore. Because they would look at you like they know four men had been intimate with you within that twelve block radius.

Allison Kugel: So you're saying women are held to a higher standard.

50 Cent (Curtis Jackson): Absolutely! This is why the Queen stands, so everyone can admire her beauty! She's more beautiful. The King just sits down and he's fat under his robe. People will respect him and fear him. But she stands so they can see her whole body, and so they can see all of her beauty. It's not a thing where you consciously say, "Fuck that, and all these bitches is hoes," and use these statements towards any and everybody that you meet. These are specific terminologies created long before rap to create a description of someone in their behavior. When it falls into the actual art form it feels offensive, and I understand there are different points. Socially, you have people that are afraid to hear that. They just aren't ready to hear it, like it should only happen while someone's having a fight, in their head. Because if you said, "You bitch!" in the middle of an argument you would understand it, and think it was because he was upset. As opposed to, you're hearing it in a record and you're feeling like, "he completely thinks I'm a second class citizen."

With two Type-A personalities champing at the bit to express our respective views, this back and forth went on for a good while before we found our way back to more general topics related to the music business and his newest projects.

But as I originally explained in this article, any debate I engage in with an interview subject has little to do with my own personal hot buttons or hurt feelings. My questions and follow up questions are about asking what I feel millions of people would want to ask, were they in the position I was in with direct access to this person. It's also about pushing for truth. What I am after in just about every interview I conduct is, not so much exposing, but revealing that person's truth to my readers. Sometimes you have to nudge someone out of their comfort zone or "off script," if you will, to get to their truth.

It's like what Talia Shire's character, Adrienne, screams to Rocky at a pivotal point in the movie, *Rocky III*. "We've got everything but the truth. *What's the truth, dammit!?*"

Look, I could interview someone who wholeheartedly believes that the sky is green and the ocean is orange. I would just want to know what makes them tick; why do they believe the sky is green and the ocean is orange? I want to then share that story with readers. It's that simple. In fact, at one point I was joking with Fifty that I wasn't legally married to my son's father because, as I put it at the time, "I don't like contracts." Of course I was being tongue in cheek and a bit edgy with my comment. I then told Fifty that my brother, Jared, the culprit sitting to his direct right, had been nagging me for ages to get married to which Fifty replied in Jared's direction, "Get out her face, man!" I broke up laughing as I shot my brother a mischievous look.

Throughout our 90 minute, yes, *90 minute* interview, we actually vibed really well and shared opinions, jokes and ideas on a number of topics. We covered everything ranging from his tumultuous parentless upbringing, his old neighborhood in Queens, his hesitance to enter into a serious romantic relationship, and his reverence for mentor and fellow rap artist Eminem aka Marshall Mathers. Regarding his high opinion of rapper Eminem, he told me:

> "I think Em is Air Jordan. I think Em is Tiger Woods... There have been other white rappers prior to him have success, but they weren't as good. So now if you put him against whoever you're calling your top emcee, there's a high probability that they get their ass whooped on the track, because he's that good."

He didn't have many positive things to say about rappers Kanye West or Jay-Z, which I chalked up to a case of sour grapes and ego *(sorry Fifty!)*. Here's how that Q/A went:

Allison Kugel: You were quoted as saying that "you're aware of Jay Z and Kanye West, but you don't care about them." Who *do* you care about? Who are your professional role models?

50 Cent (Curtis Jackson): I'm aware of a lot of people. Do I care about them? No. Do they care about me? No. I don't look up to any of them. I care about Em. I'm sure he has my best interests in mind. What people mistake is because we're in the same business, and hip hop is the kind of thing… you can't go to work in hip hop. You can't go from 9 to 5 and then go home. It's the kind of thing that you stay aware of consistently what's going on, what's working and what's not working, and who's doing what. Then from there it's territories and what you get from working with this person, or where they're going. These artists are not people that I would call at leisure just to say, "Hey, how are you doing?" They're not my friends, and I believe because we're not friends, that they don't care about what I'm doing either. So I would say openly that I couldn't care less about what they're doing.

Come to think of it, we had so much time together that there's not much we *didn't* discuss.

Perhaps what I found most intriguing and endearing about Curtis Jackson aka 50 Cent is that after he would say something of importance, he seemed to search my eyes and expression for approval, and he's very touchy feely. I don't mean in a sexual way, and I can say that with assurance since my brother was practically breathing down his neck less than a foot away. He likes to reach over and put his hand on your leg, squeeze your arm or give you a playful nudge to make his point or to illicit a reaction. I gotta admit, I thought it was cute.

A few of my favorite quotes from this interview have to do with Fifty's use of language in his music to convey some things that confused or upset him in his younger years. His ability to spin them into colorful lyrics and how he broke those lyrics down to me made me laugh. His confusion about his mother's sexual preference when he was a young boy led to the song *Love It or Hate It*. He put it to me like this:

> "'Coming up I was confused; my mama kissing a girl; confusion occurs; coming up in a cold world.' When I actually wrote that song *(Love It or Hate It)*, I was reflecting. My mom passed when I was eight, so I'm writing from a seven year old child's perspective. You don't see a seven year old child seeing it when I'm saying it. You just hear, 'Coming up I was confused...' From a child's perspective it was like, 'What's going on here? Maybe mommy is just really close to her girlfriend.'"

But I'll never forget how the lyric "I love you like a fat kid loves cake" from his hit song *21 Questions*, had us rolling in laughter as he broke down the meaning of those lyrics for me:

> 50 Cent (Curtis Jackson): When I wrote, "I love you like a fat kid loves cake," and people smile at me in the crowd, so I know that they're envisioning a fat kid eating cake when they're smiling. But what I was trying to say is, "I love you, but too much of you is no good for me."

> **Allison Kugel: It's a funny line *(laughs)*.**

> 50 Cent (Curtis Jackson): As soon as you hear it you see a fat kid, you see the cake...

> **Allison Kugel: And you see a fat kid devouring cake...**

> 50 Cent (Curtis Jackson): Right. And it's just interesting. Words are amazing!

I think I've loved every man in my life the way a fat kid loves cake. Just saying.

But anyway...

At one point we got to talking about his fans and why people, in general, seek autographs, pictures, or a moment to say, "Hi, how are you?" to him. I asked Fifty if he fully understood why people would want his autograph. The obvious answer is because he is famous, and autograph seeking is a long held tradition in our society. But I wanted his specific take on this phenomena:

Allison Kugel: Anything can be considered art, right? Where do you draw the line?

50 Cent (Curtis Jackson): Nobody's gonna pay a million dollars for me and you scribbling. They pick who to pay. "Who's scribbling are we gonna pay for?" Once they die, you're like, "Oh, wow. This is amazing!" Or, "So what do *you* see?"

Allison Kugel: Or, "What was he thinking when he scribbled that?" Like, don't you ever wonder why people want your autograph?

50 Cent (Curtis Jackson): I do, but I think it's just something that says that they met you. That physically, I was in the same space with you.

Allison Kugel: Then they put it on Ebay and make a killing.

50 Cent (Curtis Jackson): Oh, yeah, yeah. But they have to find someone else who wants it. I'll sign my jackets, my hats and stuff. I'll

> go up on stage and I'll throw them into the crowd at different points, to give the audience memorabilia from when I wore it during an actual show, and I'll put the date and where the show was at.

After a while I realized that we were talking for a long time but no one was coming out to get us, so who was I to stop the interview? The more material the better, right? Suddenly, the publicist, Yvette Gayle, came out onto the balcony with an almost panicked urgency and she was none too pleased that we had been gabbing away for close to two hours. There were a gaggle of other journalists waiting in the lobby for their time with the rapper. I feigned my apologies for us losing track of time, but secretly applauded myself for landing such a lengthy, uninterrupted interview.

At the time that this interview was published, we hadn't yet gotten in with various entertainment news syndication networks like W.E.N.N. *(World Entertainment News Network)* who could have spread our 50 Cent interview quotes far and wide, so I'm glad that they will be brought to many more people through this book.

As much as I admire Fifty as an artist and entrepreneur, I do personally think he is struggling to find his voice as an emcee these days. I don't think that his music has ascended to meet his current life circumstances, and I feel some soul searching is in order. Though I do think he is a gifted actor. I recommend a 2011 independent film he starred in about a rising football star who is diagnosed with cancer. It's called, *All Things Fall Apart*. It's a must see for his fans. And, of course, I'm addicted to the series *Power* on Starz.

Here is what Fifty had to say in 2009 about who he makes his music for:

Allison Kugel: Who are you writing for? When you're writing and recording music, who are you making the music for, in your mind?

50 Cent (Curtis Jackson): Initially, I wrote music that people could relate to in the environment. My core wants to hear the music for [them]. But if an artist has a specific demographic he's making music for, how limited is that artist? I just make music for people to appreciate at some point. If you had asked me to make a wish in 2003 it would be that people enjoy my music. That's it. That's all I wanted. From there I acquired what comes with being successful as an actual artist, and then assessed the situation and went further into business ventures that allowed me to earn more away from the music than I've earned from the actual music. But when you write these different things it's from exposure. It's from what you've developed a comfort with from things being

said around you. You're using terminologies and descriptions that make you feel like it felt in that environment. A lot of times the artist is revisiting what they've experienced until they get it 100%. I never made a remix to my best songs because they were done right to begin with. They were smash hit records. You don't revisit those records again, you go somewhere else. And no matter how hard you try, when those things have a really strong impression on the general public, you won't top it in their head.

When we were photo editing this interview I fell in love with a certain image of 50 Cent where his back is facing the camera and displays a giant "50" tattoo. I thought it made a cool statement, so counterintuitive to what we would usually put as the first picture of an interview. I chose this image to stand beside the opening paragraph.

Shortly after this article was published I received a collect telephone call from a prison inmate named James "Jimmy" Sabatino who I'd been in contact with regarding a possible article collaboration we had been tossing around at the time. Sabatino was in the media quite a bit back when he was heavily cited in the infamous 2008 Los Angeles Times expose written by Chuck Philips. In the explosive L.A. Times article, Philips revisited 1994's shooting of Tupac Shakur at New York's Quad Studios. James Sabatino was written about in the article which insinuated he was an alleged accomplice in the still unsolved shooting. The accuracy of this article has since been disputed and Chuck Philips fired from the L.A. Times.

I had mailed Sabatino a hard copy of my Fifty Cent interview weeks prior since he was incarcerated at the time and without Internet access. Weeks later I got a collect phone call from Sabatino during which he told me this was the best and most raw 50 Cent interview he had ever read. Talk about street cred.

Mugging for my iPhone. #selfienation

CHAPTER SEVEN

*"It's not like we show every last detail of
our lives… we might be perceived to show
everything on camera, but there is so much
that's just really close to us and private."*
– told to me by Kim Kardashian

Before I get into my firsthand experiences with
Kim, Khloe and Kourtney Kardashian, I feel a
little backstory and op-ed action is in order since
they seem to be such a controversial bunch. The
Kardashians illicit some really strong opinions in
both directions. So please bear with me as I explain
my own take on this.

I can remember, back in 2007/2008, when E!'s
Keeping Up With The Kardashians was still in its
infancy and the Kardashians had something of a
Generation Y and Millennial pop culture following.
I had recently developed a pretty tightknit working
relationship with the folks over at the E! Network,
particularly then head of publicity, John Rizzotti.
Having interviewed E! News Anchor Giuliana Rancic
for the first time in January of 2008, followed by
their new late night personality at the time, Chelsea
Handler, we had a great thing going. In February

of that same year, John and I had decided that we really liked working together. It was around this time that my editor, Jason Manheim, and I began having the "should we or shouldn't we" conversation about whether or not to pursue any of the Kardashians for interviews.

Another wrinkle, during my interview with Chelsea Handler, John was hanging out on the telephone line when I asked Chelsea if she thought that Kim Kardashian's infamous sex tape had been leaked on purpose. After my interview with Chelsea wrapped up, I got an email from John imploring me not to bash Kim in my Chelsea piece, but to please "be gentle" as Kim was "part of the E! family." I actually felt terrible and I called John and apologized for causing him agida over the whole thing. You have to remember that at the end of 2007, and beginning of 2008, the sex tape was the centerpiece of the media hype surrounding Kim & co.

I promised to omit my sex tape comments about Kim from the Chelsea Handler interview, to which John said, "Then consider it water under the bridge."

We enjoyed a great working relationship together from that point on. The truth is, it was never my intention to bash Kim Kardashian, but rather I wanted to get Chelsea's take on the then recent phenomenon of the Kardashians' sudden fame. I was essentially just being a journalist. But as the years went on, I became more and more creative at uncovering important information without placing my interview subjects directly in the hot seat. I developed my *method* for creating quotable celebrity interviews that generated a lot of secondary media coverage, often leaving many of my colleagues in the dust. Celebrity Journalism is an art form. It's about bringing a person's humanity to the surface for readers, without making the interview subject feel threatened or putting them on the defensive, if it's done right.

Yeah, Kim and her family were beginning to get pretty famous, but like any celebrity who's launched from a scandal, you question the validity of their presence on the celebratory map. After all, what were we all celebrating them for, exactly? I felt the same way everyone else did about this subject matter at the time. I also felt conflicted about promoting the idea that you can become a success and be rewarded for making a sex tape. My fears have been proven correct with the subsequent slew of copycat sex tape pseudo-celebrities that popped up everywhere. Everyone from Laurence Fishburne's daughter, Montana Fishburne, to former MTV *Teen Mom* star Farrah Abraham, and even NBA star Kris Humphries's ex-girlfriend, Myla Sinanaj, have all gotten in on the "act" so-to-speak. They've all hoped to strike gold through the release of a "leaked sex tape."

Here's the rub on this issue. I don't blame Kim Kardashian for any of this. I really feel that she did a brilliant job of turning lemons into lemonade and re-branding herself as a Hollywood "It" girl, and let's face it, a thriving international brand. Like it or lump it, she is a financial and commercial success story. And, no, at this point I do not believe that she leaked her sex tape on purpose. Though even if she did, that is between her and her higher power. I don't judge any human being walking this earth. I have enough on my plate.

When people would ask me why I continued to interview the Kardashians over the years, *and they asked a lot*, my answer was always the same. "As long as you are watching their television shows, buying magazines that feature them on the cover and Googling them, I am obliged as a journalist to cover them." Fair deal?

I've never felt the kind of animosity towards anyone that I have seen hurled at the Kardashian/Jenner family on the Internet. I don't really understand it. But here is what I can assess based on some anecdotal research I've done in the blogosphere comment sections. People appear to be angry with Kim Kardashian and Kris Jenner because they set out to become rich and famous and they succeeded. In other words, they knew how to work the media to achieve their desired ends. Apparently that offends people.

My journalistic journey with the three Kardashian sisters began when I first interviewed Khloe Kardashian. It was early 2009, and the family had two seasons of *KUWTK* under their belts. They were currently promoting the third season of their now decade-long hit reality show. I was pregnant at the time and I had canceled on Khloe at the 11th hour on the day of what was scheduled to be our first interview together. As the morning progressed I was dealing with stress and putting out multiple fires at work, and my belly began to feel uncomfortable. That discomfort then turned to pain. I was about five months along in my pregnancy, and of course feared the worst. I called Khloe's then-publicist and told her I had to reschedule. I spent the rest of that day in bed, feet up, as per my doctor's orders. When I spoke with Khloe the very next day, all she seemed concerned about was how I was feeling, and was I ok? Did I know if I was having a boy or a girl, and all of the stuff that girls talk about when there is any mention of a pregnancy.

I apologized to her for canceling on her at the last minute the previous day, and she countered, "Are you kidding? Your health is what matters. That's a lot more important than me!" I remember Khloe being somewhat misrepresented on the first few seasons of *KUWTK*, as this acerbic and sarcastic instigator of the bunch. As much as I've seen behind the curtain throughout my journalism and public relations career, I still sometimes become misled by media representations just like everyone else does. My guard was up as I began to speak with Khloe for the first time. But when she showed genuine concern and interest for how I was feeling, it disarmed me. Isn't this thing supposed to work the other way around?

Our conversation eventually bled into her initial hesitance to be on television. When her mom, Kris Jenner, and *KUWTK* producer, Ryan Seacrest, approached the rest of the family to take a stab at letting cameras into their everyday lives for the E! Network, Khloe wasn't so sure. She told me that she and Kourtney were gun shy at first, mainly due to their witnessing some of their childhood friends, including Nicole Richie and Paris Hilton, lose their privacy and deal with some unwelcome rumors and gossip. Here is how Khloe put it to me at the time:

> "I've grown up in the industry. My best friend was Nicole Richie growing up, and we went to school with the Hiltons. I've grown up around all of these people. It's never been something that I really searched for or ever wanted. To do *Keeping Up With The Kardashians*, I had to really be talked into it."

A scarring point for Khloe was having a front row seat for the O.J. Simpson trial and subsequent media circus of the mid-nineties in which her mother's best friend, the late Nicole Brown Simpson, was brutally murdered. Her father, the late attorney and businessman, Robert Kardashian, was on the defense team for the Kardashians' former family friend, O.J. Simpson:

> "From living through the O.J. Simpson trial with my dad, the press was always so horrible. So from my experience, it's always been bad. I [was] happy in my little niche, running my store. Kim and I were styling for a bunch of celebrities, so we were personal shoppers and stuff. I was very comfortable doing what I was doing."

At the time, I had to ask about their Klan's propensity for all sharing the same initials:

Allison Kugel: Did you ever ask your mom why she named all of her daughters with the first initial "K"?

Khloe Kardashian: I never did. But my mom's name is Kristen, and we call her Kris. And her sister's name is Karen. I've never asked her that, that's a good question. When Nicole Simpson passed away, that was one of my mom's best friends, my mom wanted to name Kendall, Nicole. We were all like, "No!" because she should continue the Ks. But Kendall's middle name is Nicole.

When I re-read this interview from February 2009, while putting this book together, I couldn't help but think about all that Khloe has had to deal with in the press in recent years, regarding her marriage to Lamar Odom and tabloid stories about her late father. I know that many wonderful opportunities have come her way as a result of *KUWTK*, but I wonder if she ever regrets her decision to agree to do the show.

Khloe and I also discussed her getting a DUI during filming of the first season of the show. I know that she was horrified and embarrassed by this mistake, particularly since the family, at that time, was still reeling from the untimely drug-related death of another good family friend, Brent Shapiro *(late son of famed defense attorney, Robert Shapiro)*. She swore to me that I would never again read about her being charged with another DUI. She had learned her lesson. I can often tell when a celebrity is lying to me during an interview. Based on circumstances, I make the judgment whether or not to call them on it. In this case I was pretty confident that Khloe was being truthful and genuine.

I also reprimanded Khloe *(in a lighthearted way)* about their lack of security at their DASH store in Calabasas, California. At the time they were all still actually working at the store and still getting accustomed to their fame. I told Khloe that anyone, at any time, could simply walk into their boutique and cause a problem for them. She giggled, but I think I drove my point home. Of course, now, the Kardashians are swimming in security detail.

The real drama unfolded after this interview had already taken place, at press time. At the time of the interview, Kim's then-boyfriend, Reggie Bush, had introduced Khloe to NBA player, Rashad McCants. Khloe seemed excited about her new relationship with Rashad. I asked her some questions about their relationship and she told me they had "gotten serious." We saw no harm in adding a red carpet image of Khloe and Rashad into our photo editing to correspond with her comments about him.

No sooner did the interview post and work its way into the search engines, Khloe announced her split from Rashad McCants amid his cheating admission and him telling her that he had been with her to boost his career. I'm not thrilled that their picture together is forever in that article, but what are you going do? It's not like I was some fortune teller or something. Apparently neither was Khloe.

My parting words for Khloe Kardashian at the end of this first interview were that I strongly felt she was being misrepresented on *KUWTK* in the editing room. Her personality is a lot more accommodating and much softer than she was originally portrayed on the show. I'm happy that they tend to show more of that side of her these days.

My next interview was with Kourtney Kardashian in August of 2009 when she and Khloe were promoting their inaugural season of *Kourtney & Khloe Take Miami*. This interview was booked directly through my buddy John Rizzotti over at the E! Network. There was a lot riding on this press tour for Kourtney. This would be her and Khloe's first foray into branding themselves as viable ratings draws for the E! Network, apart from the hype surrounding Kim. In addition, the stakes were high for another reason that I was partly kept in the dark about during the time of my interview with Kourtney. At the time, the world thought that Kourtney and Scott Disick were kaput. In reality, Kourtney was pregnant with Scott's baby *(why do I feel like I'm writing about a soap opera here?)*. But here is where it got interesting. I had recently given birth to my son, Marcus, who was now nearly three months old. I happened to ask Kourtney about the children's clothing collections that her and her mom, Kris, sold at their now closed children's boutique, *Smooch*. Somehow the conversation turned to pregnancy, labor and giving birth.

I mentioned to Kourtney that when I had interviewed Khloe I told her that I was scared of giving birth.

That's when Kourtney said:

"How was it? I feel like it's terrifying."

There was something about the way she asked me; it made me take pause and wonder what was up. But why would I ever think she might have a bun in the oven? We even talked about epidural versus no epidural and she asked me about my experience with natural childbirth. A little later on in our conversation I sniffed around, mentioning that I had peeped her MySpace page *(we're going back to 2009)* and her status read "in a relationship." There was silence for a beat and then she said, "Oh, because that page is so old." Yeah, Kourtney told me some little white lies, ok *big* white lies. The media reveal about her reuniting with Scott and being pregnant hadn't taken place yet. I noticed that she wore baggy black ensembles to events soon after our interview took place, stuff that looked way too matronly for red carpet appearances. At the very end of her media tour, Kourtney debuted her baby bump to longtime family friend Kathie Lee Gifford on *The Today Show*.

No, I'm not peeved about missing the big scoop. Ok, maybe a little bit.

While Khloe is sharp, funny and opinionated *(which I love)* and Kim is sweet natured, out of the three of them Kourtney is the one I could most see hanging out with socially. Our interview was cute and campy; lighthearted fare. Kourtney seemed to me to be the least interested in her celebrity of all three of the Kardashian sisters. It seemed to me like her celeb status is just another accessory she puts on when she has to promote something associated with the Kardashian brand. But it's far from who she is.

Kourtney is kind of self-deprecating and she's a big second-guesser when it comes to decision making.

She said to me:

> *"I like to get advice from a lot of different people, and I think it's really annoying because I ask everyone, and then you involve everyone in your stuff."*

I found Kourtney to be very grounded and down-to-earth. Her valley girl twang is actually kind of misleading, because as people can see in recent years, life for her is all about family, health and motherhood. It's been fun to watch her really flourish and come into her own as a mother, which is a role she seems quite confident in.

Though Khloe's least favorite part of filming a reality show is negative and hurtful media coverage, Kourtney told me that her least favorite part was getting captured on film with her foot in her mouth. Here's what she had to say to me about that:

> "I used to be really bad when we first started filming, like, [self-] conscious of what I would say and just thinking, 'Ugh! I said this, it's so dumb!'

or 'I said this, it's so crazy!' But I think that after watching the show, so little of it actually airs of what we film. Because we film 12-18 hours a day almost seven days a week, so not that much of it shows."

Kourtney's above statement to me is not to be missed. If you re-read the above quote, you'll realize that out of 84 plus hours of film shot in a week, only a snippet here and a snippet there actually airs. The show's editors then get ahold of the chosen footage and arrange it as they please, complete with soundtrack and special effects to keep the viewer visually stimulated and engaged throughout each episode.

After my interview with Kourtney was published, she blogged about it on her website at KourtneyKardashian.com, Here is the intro part of what Kourtney posted at the time:

"I recently did an interview with Allison Kugel at PR.com. We talked about the Dash stores, my love of Miami, Bruce's affinity for DIY, and more! Thanks Allison for a great interview!"

December of 2009 was the first time I interviewed Kim Kardashian.

My interview with Kim came to me courtesy of personal publicist Jill Fritzo over at PMK.BNC (she has since started her own firm, Jill Fritzo Public

Relations), a popular PR firm among artists and media personalities, and E!'s own publicist John Rizzotti (who has since moved on to CBS television), who were both becoming part of my regular celebrity journalism posse by this point.

I was told that I would be meeting up with Kim backstage at the *Today Show* at 30 Rockefeller Plaza in New York, and that's all I was told. That damn building is so big with so many mazes, and as I learned that morning, has multiple greenrooms. I was like a mouse searching for a piece of cheese. I peeped my head into different areas by different shows until I finally found the correct greenroom after about 45 minutes of frantic searching. One of my biggest pet peeves is tardiness and I'm just as hard on myself about being on time as I am with others. I can't stand to be late... *for anything*. If I say I will be somewhere at 10AM, you can bet I will be there by 9:59, especially when it comes to business matters. Luckily, I arrived before Kim and Jill did.

The *Today Show* greenroom was bustling with hair and makeup people; talent sitting in chairs getting primped before going on camera; assistants running in all directions; producers briefing talent on upcoming segments; security people; and random friends of this one or that one. While I waited, Kathie Lee Gifford blew through the greenroom in a whirlwind on her way back to the *Today* set, Donny Deutsch chatted with a friend about his precious "baby" dog, and different *Today* show guests looked excited to be making an appearance on the show to plug whatever they were there to promote. I sat on the couch half-heartedly watching the television monitor and inconspicuously eavesdropping on various conversations. Finally Kim, Jill, and Khloe came rushing through the greenroom to get settled before going on-air. I was surprised to see Khloe at first, but remembered that the girls usually promoted their shows in at least pairs of two. Kourtney was extremely pregnant with her son Mason at the time, and was likely sticking close to home in Los Angeles.

I spotted them, caught Kim's and Jill's eyes and said a "Hello." Kim promptly squealed back an overly enthusiastic "*Hiii!!*" as if she had trained herself to *turn on* whenever anyone who might be of any consequence was in close proximity. That was my very first impression.

My first interview with Khloe had been on the phone, so this was my first time meeting her face-to-face. Her long toned legs and overall attractive appearance were striking to me. Television and pictures don't really do her any justice.

As quickly as Kim and Khloe arrived in the greenroom, that's how quickly they were ushered out and onto the set to chat up Kathie Lee Gifford and Hoda Kotb. Jill told me I would sit down with the girls for our interview after they finished up with Kathie Lee and Hoda. I flopped back down onto the couch, watched more television and wondered how long I could continue to keep myself occupied before going a little stir crazy in that room. Back then I had a BlackBerry, so I couldn't occupy myself with Google News, Instagram and all of that.

What's exciting to the everyday person walking the street is lost on me when I'm focused on the task at hand. Before an interview, *any interview*, I am solely focused on how to bring out the most interesting aspects of the person, and how to pull the best information for good story angles. That was my job.

If I were about to interview then-President Obama, the only thing on my mind prior to sitting down on set would be, "How can I ask this question about his Affordable Care Act in a way that no other journalist has yet?" Once the interview is over and I'm back in the car, then I'll freak out about meeting the president. Or, oftentimes I'll develop a headache after an interview due to all of the pent up nervous adrenaline that I suppressed before and during the interview, itself.

No, I'm not comparing the Kardashians to the president of the United States *(please don't nail me on that one)*.

When Jill brought Kim and Khloe back into the greenroom after their television appearance, Kim and I sat down next to each other on the greenroom's couch, Khloe took a seat in a chair right next to the couch, and Jill sat behind us, sort of peering over from time to time in between checking her phone.

I took a car service into the city on this morning and I happened to have this anal- retentive driver who continuously called my phone and text messaged me throughout the interview. I had to repeatedly hit the "Ignore" button on my phone while trying to zero in on what Kim and Khloe were saying to me.

I was furious at the constant distraction. I love Khloe but I wasn't expecting a joint interview, so my questions that I'd prepared were really geared towards Kim. They were written for a one-on-one interview. I needed to quickly shift gears, and thank God for Khloe, because I didn't get much meat from Kim on this particular morning. By that, I don't mean that I was looking to clobber her over the head with a fire round of probing and invasive questions, but I'm a big conversationalist and like to put my two cents in on just about any topic you could throw at me: religion, politics, sex, shopping, relationships, spirituality… I've got strong opinions on all of 'em! Khloe is like that as well. Kim, not so much. She has a more go-with-the-flow kind of vibe. Actually, to put it more accurately, she has a media face that tends to lean towards politically correct.

At one point in the conversation I reached over to Kim and blatantly asked, "Am I making you uncomfortable?" To which Kim replied in a high-pitched baby doll tone,

"No, not at all." I looked over at Khloe and shrugged as if to say, "Well, I had to ask." Kim then mentioned something about jetlag due to a red eye flight from LA to New York the previous night into the early morning. She even threw in a wide-mouthed yawn for good measure.

All in all, I found Kim to be pretty guarded with me and when I would direct a question her way, she would look straight ahead, take a couple of beats to gather her thoughts, and then recite an answer that she likely deemed beneficial or neutral to her growing brand. It didn't come across as particularly authentic or off-the-cuff. But in her defense, I think that she was on a mission *at that time* to come across as well-spoken and sophisticated in the hopes of putting more distance between herself and her sex tape beginnings. Khloe, on the other hand, loves answering questions and is always game to say what is on her mind. Kim hung on to what Khloe said and looked for ways to jump in with an opinion here and there.

At the time of this interview, Kim was newly back together with NFL player Reggie Bush and Khloe had just tied the knot with Lamar Odom. My eyes kept diverting to two distinct places. I couldn't help but look at Khloe's humongous ring *(it was gorgeous!)*, highlighted by a cursive *"LO"* tattoo on her left hand; Lamar Odom's initials. I also kept looking at Kim's face which I noticed barely made a movement or expression as she spoke. Her face was beautiful and impeccably made up. Sculpted cheekbones, exotically-shaped eyes and almond-toned skin surrounded by lush dark brunette waves of hair. Ironically, her most famous ASSet didn't look nearly as big as I expected it would, at least in the outfit she had on that day. Although she was wearing all black, including a black blazer. But her facial expressions were non-existent and I thought, "Oh no, Botox? Why?" I mean, why would someone think they need Botox at the age of 29? That was her age at that time. I just don't get it, but maybe that's because I don't live in Hollyweird.

When Kim first sat down next to me she placed her Hermes Birkin Bag on the floor next to my handmade, patchwork tote bag that I bought for $40.00 at a local craft fair on Long Island. She gave my much less expensive label-free bag a once over and shot it a look of pity, or maybe it was a look that said, "Your bag's not cool enough to hang out with my bag." I just wasn't into fashion or labels at the time. I'm still not overly thrilled with the world of elite fashion items that cost a mint, though I have loosened up and indulged a bit more in the past few years.

Kim was game to openly discuss body image and her recent weight loss with me. Here's what she had to say to me back in December of 2009 about her body, and how then-boyfriend, Reggie Bush, felt about her famous figure:

"I definitely have toned up so much. I've gotten into really good shape. And I even asked my boyfriend, I said, 'Babe, all the comments are saying that I'm too skinny. Ugh! They were calling me fat before, and now I'm too skinny. What do you like better?' And he was like, 'You look amazing!' Before, I was insecure. I'd cover my arms and I'd try and figure out different outfits to cover up certain body parts that I wasn't comfortable with. Now I feel confident and comfortable, and I feel like I'm in the best shape of my life. So it's not just about being skinny. It's more about being in better shape. Before I had no muscle tone, no definition. Now I'm just in really great shape. I'm living a healthier lifestyle, so I'm really happy with that. And I'm still really curvy."

And yes, all of those mean spirited comments posted on blogs and other websites about the girls *did* hurt their feelings at the time. To tell you the truth I don't know how I would ever handle it. I don't personally know what it feels like, and chances are if you're a civilian reading this book, neither do you. But I would imagine that it's something like mean high school gossip… times a million. Ouch! Next time you're feeling the impulse to type something mean into a comment box, think about that for a moment.

When I brought up all of the horrible things Kim and Khloe have read about themselves online they had this to say at the time:

Allison Kugel: Do you guys read all of the comments that are written about you all over the Internet?

Khloe Kardashian: I never do.

Kim Kardashian: I try not to, but I read Twitter. So I knew what people were saying on Twitter.

Khloe Kardashian: I read Twitter, but I never read comments. They're never nice!

Kim Kardashian: Comments are for people that have nothing better to do.

Khloe Kardashian: One time years ago I read comments and I was like, "Do they say this just about us or about everyone?" People say bad things about Megan Fox, and the most gorgeous people! How could you criticize them?! So it doesn't matter who you are or what you do. You could be the most famous person in the world. They're still going to talk shit about you.

Allison Kugel: It bothers me when I look at it because I think, "Is there that much negative energy in the world?" It's depressing.

Kim Kardashian: Oh, completely.

Khloe Kardashian: That's why I don't read that stuff, because even if you don't believe it, it sits in the back of your head.

Kim Kardashian: You just have to try to ignore it or not read the comments.

Kim and Khloe are used to being asked about their reality shows, their style, their men, their looks, but rarely anything political. I was genuinely curious to know if they were existing in a celebrity bubble or if they were at all in touch with the pressing issues going on in our world. I brought up some outside-the-box topics by asking Kim if she followed politics at all. It was like I turned off her light switch. She just wasn't all that interested, uttering an obligatory:

"I just recently watched [Obama's] speech on the war and sending 30,000 more troops. I follow it here and there."

I then decided to get a little more broad with my line of questioning, hoping it would illicit some more depth. I asked Kim:

"Who would you like to meet, and why?"

I wasn't expecting her to say the Dalai Lama or former Secretary of State, Madeleine Albright, but here's what I got:

Kim Kardashian: I would like to meet George Clooney... because he's so cute.

Khloe Kardashian: Cute answer. I would want to meet Obama.

Kim Kardashian: Just because he's Obama!

One thing that stood out to me during this particular interview was Khloe's passion for using her public platform to help further the efforts of the gay rights movement and the legalization of gay marriage.

Here are some of Khloe's observations about gay rights laws in the state of Florida, or lack thereof:

"If you were living with someone for over a certain amount of years you weren't allowed to be claimed on their insurance policy [in Florida]. Florida is a really segregated state when it comes to sexuality. You don't think so because of Miami, but any place outside of Miami is very segregated. Miami Beach is such a bubble. To me, it just meant a lot because I have so many friends that are gay. And my mom, when we were younger, had so many friends that were gay. Love is love. It's not promoting anything negative in my opinion. They just want to love someone, so who are we to say that they can't."

In total, our chat lasted about half an hour and then I glanced at Jill who smirked and gave me the universal "wrap it up" sign by rotating her two pointer fingers in a barrel spin. As I caught up with Jill after the interview, Khloe joked that she was glad to finally put a face to the pregnant chick on the other end of the phone whom she spoke with a year earlier *(moi)*, and Kim offered up an, "It was nice to meet you."

For my end, I could have been much warmer and more sociable at that point, but for some reason, I wasn't. I think I was a bit distracted because I just wanted to get into my car and get home to my son, who was only seven months old at the time. I dealt with typical working mom guilt just like every other working mother in the universe.

And, in case you are wondering, here is the difference between a non-famous person who works in the entertainment industry versus a famous person working in the entertainment industry:

I beat Kim, Khloe and Jill out the door and onto the street right outside 30 Rock where my driver was pulling up to collect me. I told my then-boyfriend,

Patrick, that I was on my way back to Long Island as I began to meander over to my waiting car. Before I got to my car, I see Kim, Khloe and Jill step out onto the same street as me, only the scene unfolded much differently for them. No sooner did they hit the street, someone yelled out, "It's Kim Kardashian!" The pedestrian then hopped in front of Kim, wrapped her arm around Kim with a phone in hand, and began snapping away. Less than a minute later, more and more people crowded around, jumping next to and in front of Kim and snapping pictures of her, and with her, as if she were on display in Madame Tussaud's Wax Museum. Except she wasn't the wax figure version of herself, she was the real live breathing human version of herself. I actually have to give her credit. She handled the madness with ease and grace, and accommodated everyone she could as she made her way to her car.

Nobody called out Khloe's name as she walked right beside Kim, and I wondered how Khloe felt about that. It's not to say that Khloe's not extremely recognizable, but while there was *Kimsanity* on the streets outside of 30 Rock, Khloe's celebrity status took a back seat.

Fast forward to June of 2011 when I get another call from my good friend John over at E!. John let me know that Kim was doing a round of interviews to promote the latest season of *KUWTK*, and do I want in? I booked a slot on her media tour, and I was told to focus my line of questioning mainly on the show since Kim had an exclusive deal in place with *People* Magazine to officially announce her ill-fated engagement to NBA basketball player, Kris Humphries.

During this interview, Kim was a little more jovial and relaxed. Her answers to my questions seemed more honest, though she is still kind of a controlled person who is conscious of her brand at all times. She's not one to just develop spontaneous diarrhea of the mouth.

The first thing I asked her this time was whether or not she would be taking Kris Humphries' last name once they were married. She gave me the same answer that she recently gave another reporter before her nuptials to Kanye West. She told me she would be changing her name to Kim Kardashian Humphries. For some reason, this was some big scoop at the time and was picked up by *OK!* Magazine and added to Kim's Wikipedia page *(it's long since been removed from Wikipedia for obvious reasons)*. It never ceases to amaze me what the media finds newsworthy. I even got unfairly accused by my editor of leaking the quote to *OK!* Magazine to promote myself apart from my media outlet at the time, PR.com. I didn't even know anyone who worked at *OK!* Magazine. People took excerpts from my interviews all the time and did with them what they wanted.

Kim was excited to tell me that her younger sister, Khloe, had recently met and briefly made small talk with President Obama, during which the president allegedly complimented Khloe on the family's reality show, *Keeping Up With The Kardashians*. Kim was nervous to be quoted about what was actually spoken between Khloe and President Obama since she couldn't remember the exact words that were exchanged.

Here's an excerpt from that part of our interview:

Allison Kugel: Who is the most unlikely celebrity fan of *Keeping Up With The Kardashians* that you've encountered? What celebrity has approached you to tell you they were a fan of the show and you were shocked by it?

Kim Kardashian: That's a good question. We'll get that and we're like, "Oh my God!" like, we wouldn't even think that these people would know who we are. Probably I would say President Obama, when he said something to Khloe.

Allison Kugel: President Obama told Khloe he was a fan of *Keeping Up With The Kardashians*?

Kim Kardashian: I mean, he didn't say those exact words, but he said, "Nice show," or something along those lines. Or something like, "I like the show." I would have to ask Khloe so don't quote me on that.

***Allison Kugel: And Khloe came back and
reported that to everyone?***

Kim Kardashian: Yeah, she was like, "Oh my God! I
just met the President and he said… bla bla bla!"

During another point in our conversation I asked Kim
what her late father, Robert Kardashian, would have
thought of her then-fiancé, Kris Humphries. I found
it curious at the time that she didn't have a whole lot
to say about Kris in response to my question. She
struggled to think of how to describe Kris or what she
loved about him. Here's what she eventually offered
in response:

> "Oh, I think he would absolutely love [Kris], because
> he's just really funny and just a good person, and
> you can tell. And the fact that he's a Christian, I
> think that he would just really, really like him."

Notice how these days, when she is asked about her
feelings for husband Kanye West, she has a lot to say.
She could talk about how amazing she thinks he is
for days. At the time I chalked it up to her wanting to
keep her private life private, but this is Kim Kardashian
we're talking about. As even Kim has been quoted as
saying, "I just love sharing my life."

One big change I noticed in Kim (*and, granted, this
was prior to the media shit storm she went through
after separating from Kris Humphries*) was that she

had a more lighthearted attitude about false tabloid stories and media gossip than she did during our previous interview. Back in 2009, when the topic of false stories came up in conversation she actually grew sullen and annoyed and said to me, "They'll take anybody's story and it's just not fair!"

During our second interview, here is what she had to say about the tabloids:

Allison Kugel: Of all of the stories you read about yourself in the celebrity weeklies, what percentage of it is true?

Kim Kardashian: I would say fifty/fifty. There are stories that are zero percent true and then there's other stories about us liking a certain nail polish color, or we're at a certain restaurant, and a lot of that stuff is true, the little stuff. Most of the big stories are just completely not true.

Allison Kugel: The stuff that is written about your relationships with one another...

Kim Kardashian: Yeah, like that we don't get along. And there was one recent story that said we were all tormented by body issues and we were all getting different [plastic] surgeries, the whole family! And we were like, "Is this a joke?!" We just laugh. You should see our chain emails, because our

> publicist will always give us a heads up the day before. The things Khloe will write, or that we'll all write, like, "Did we at least get a group discount?" We'll just totally laugh about it together.

Though Kim was sweet and we had a fun conversation this time around, she did lie through her teeth about planning to televise her wedding to Kris Humphries. I asked her if she would follow Khloe's lead and wed on television for the E! cameras. Her answer:

> "Um… don't know yet."

I wanted to scream at her, "Liar, liar, pants on fire!" But I had to maintain some professional decorum. What people don't understand about the celebrity journalism business *(and it is a business)* is that sometimes when you're dealing with a large network like E!, or any other television network for that matter, they will often have a publicist sit in on the interview. Television publicity is most notorious for this tactic. They are quick to interrupt you if you probe too deeply in a direction that they don't want you to go in. Big brother is watching and you have to pick and choose your battles. If you want the celebrity you're interviewing to open up about one thing, sometimes you have to roll over on something else. You have to create positive rapport with the celebrity, manage your professional relationship with the network people and publicists, and find that unique news angle for your interview. Talk about a balancing act!

After this interview with Kim took place, it occurred to me that I'd forgotten to ask a certain question which I felt was important to fully round out my article. The question was this:

> "Where do you place things like beauty, fashion and material goods on your list of personal priorities in life?"

I felt strongly that it was important so I shot over an email to John at E!, asking if he could email the question to Kim and shoot me back an answer that I could insert into the finished piece.

I got a reply email from John that Kim had declined to answer that specific question. I wrote back to John and quipped, "I guess that question was unfavorable." To which he responded, "You're right HA HA." My next retort back to him:

> "Ah, the life of a journalist!"

To this day, I don't get why Kim wouldn't answer that question. I don't see it as a negative thing against her brand at all. It would have offered insight into her priorities, and in my opinion, would have provided her with a great platform in which to make herself sound well-rounded and to spin some PR gold. I feel most connected to people who aren't afraid to be vulnerable and to show their humanity. Unfortunately, I never really got that from Kim.

Sometimes you have to say "Cheese!"

CHAPTER EIGHT

*"Try turning on the radio while you're having a
shower. Try that. I guarantee you'll sing."
- told to me by Tony Okungbowa, deejay from
the Ellen Show*

In the early summer of 2006 PR.com was just
beginning to get its sea legs. We'd developed a
few valuable showbiz relationships with well-known
public relations firms and with companies like VH1.
People were slowly but surely taking a chance on us
and we were having some forward movement; of
course not fast enough for my taste. I always want
things *yesterday*. At this point we were certainly
hearing "No" more than we heard "Yes" and we
were still recipients of the publicist "swap-out." And
yes, I have created much of my own lingo to combat
annoying Hollywood jargon that most people in the
entertainment industry are forced to adopt. I refuse.
I use terms that correlate more to my down-to-earth
northeastern roots and my family's professional
roots in the tire business.

I contacted a publicist over at BWR *(short for Baker
Winokur Ryder, a big deal PR firm on both coasts)*,

I believe to request an interview with actor, Omar Epps, who was starring on the hit show, *House* at the time. We were re-propositioned with a counter offer to interview the resident deejay on *The Ellen DeGeneres Show*, DJ Tony O, or Tony Okungbowa. I knew the *Ellen* show was a huge hit and I also knew that she had a deejay on her show, but I never paid too much attention beyond that. At this point in time, we were only about a year old and we were game to talk to anyone who was doing anything substantial in entertainment. I agreed to take the interview.

When my interview with Tony began I found him to be a little stuffy and seriously lacking a sense of humor. He had just resigned from *Ellen (his first resignation of two)* to embark on a serious acting career. At the time he had only been Ellen's sidekick for three years *(2003 – 2006)*, and personally, I thought he was nuts to jump off that gravy train so soon. Show business is hard, and when that right wave finally comes along you ride it to the shoreline.

As we discussed Tony's desire to leave his television post behind for an acting career, he cited Sidney Poitier as a professional inspiration and signpost that he would use to help navigate his own acting career. I told him that Ellen was probably bummed to see him leave her show so soon. In between questions that covered his fledgling acting career, which he very much liked answering, I peppered him with more lighthearted and comical questions to try and spice up this interview with some humor and gossip. Nothing mean-spirited, just some meat for readers to sink their teeth into.

People wanted to read about how much fun it was to work right beside Ellen DeGeneres and all of the cool perks that came with it. He just didn't seem to get it, and every time I cracked a joke or tried to draw him in with some personal information about myself he seemed lost as if he was in a country where he didn't speak the language. Finally, in exasperation, I began to flirt it up a bit with this Nigerian Brit to try to loosen him up until he finally blurted out, "Wait, are we doing an interview now or flirting?" Thanks Skipper, for finally catching on to my tactics. Only I wasn't flirting with *him*, per se. I was flirting with my interview subject to get that metal rod dislodged from you know where.

To get a little fun banter going I jumped right in and answered his question, cryptically. "Isn't it the same thing?" I offered. Then the ball got rolling, sort of. Here is an excerpt from my interview with Tony Okungbowa where I managed to drag him "off message" a bit:

Allison Kugel: Speaking of that, are you dating anyone?

Tony Okungbowa: No, I'm single right now.

Allison Kugel: Are you looking for a girlfriend out there in L.A.?

Tony Okungbowa: Am I looking for love? Yeah, in all the wrong places!

Allison Kugel: Laughs.

Tony Okungbowa: But still looking, you know. When it comes, it comes. I haven't found her yet.

(Tony is speaking with me from a waxing salon in Los Angeles)

I told you where I am… so all these women are coming in to get waxed and I'm checking them out as they're walking in.

Allison Kugel: Oh boy.

Tony Okungbowa: Oh, I'm teasing.

Allison Kugel: *(Laughs)* **You know what, seriously, you're sitting in a great place right now to meet someone.**

Tony Okungbowa: Ummm… in a waxing salon? Women don't come here looking for men; they're just here to get some hair off their body.

Allison Kugel: But can I tell you something… you know they're well groomed.

Tony Okungbowa: That's funny.

By this point we had covered a lot already, so Tony asked me if we could turn off the tape recorder and just talk, person-to-person. I said, "Sure." I had no idea where he was going with this.

I turned off my tape recorder, assured him that it was off and said, "So, what's up?" in a casual and curious tone. He responded by observing that once we were "off the record" he felt a palpable shift in my whole demeanor.

"Your voice and your whole energy feels different now," he commented. To which I agreed, "Yeah, I guess you're right." I was still finding my journalistic voice. At that time, barely a year into my career, I borrowed my persona from a blended cocktail of Larry King, Howard Stern and Oprah. Hey, I was 100% self-taught. Where else was I going to learn?

Years later, my "on" and "off" personalities would become seamless as I strived to be authentic in all areas of my life. Back then, not as much I guess. It would be a year later, at the age of thirty-two, that I would discover spiritual education which would turn my whole life perception completely on its head, and for the better.

We spoke on the phone, just as Tony and Allison, for about twenty minutes. It was the usual back and forth that people do when they are feeling each other out for a potential date. I can remember him asking me to describe myself and I said something like, "I'm pretty complex." To which he replied, "Ok, bring it. Let's hear…" There was a lot of that back and forth kind of stuff.

Towards the end of our phone conversation he made a point of telling me that he was giving me his email address because he trusted my ability to be discreet, or something like that, and would I please email him a picture of myself while we were still on the phone. It irked me a bit when he acted like giving me his email address was like giving away gold, but I shot him over a pic anyway.

Here's the thing, and maybe it's because I've met so many famous, semi-famous and pseudo-famous people at this point; I just don't hear all of the bells and whistles that I used to. And I flat out refuse to treat anyone better or worse than anyone else. In my book, we're all just people muddling through this earthly plane as best as we can. If you don't like it, you know where you can stick it.

We also exchanged phone numbers. Tony mentioned that he would be in New York for the week to attend and deejay at the CFDA Awards, the "Oscars of Fashion," and would I like to get together? We made plans, and in the interim I was really pre-occupied getting ready to move from my Upper East Side apartment back to Long Island, my cozy comfort zone in this world. Tony called me a handful of times, mainly to inquire about how his article was coming along in the editing process and sort of trying to gauge if I was going to portray him in a positive light. I assured him that my integrity and reputation were everything to me as a journalist, and that I would write a fair and balanced piece on him. After all, our interview was fun and filled with humorous moments once I got him going. I also respected his career as well as his cultured manner. From our few phone conversations I felt that perhaps he was someone I could become friends with, more than anything else.

When the day of our first planned date arrived, it came and went and we never went out. In Tony's defense, if memory serves, he did call or text to cancel. After we re-scheduled a day or so later… he cancelled again. By our third try at getting together he asked me where I would like to go and I replied, "I don't really know. I haven't given it much thought because I didn't know if we would actually keep our plans this time." I didn't think what I said was all that outlandish, but he really took offense. He told me that I didn't have a very good attitude. But it wasn't a big deal to me either way, frankly.

He then mentioned something about all of the inclement weather messing up his schedule. There had been quite a lot of rain in New York, so it made some sense. He then dropped this one on me: "Come on, give a brother another chance!"

Since he was coming from the city and I was now living out on Long Island, we decided we would meet up in the town of Great Neck, which is roughly 25 minutes east of Manhattan. I picked Tony up at the Long Island Railroad train station in Great Neck, we parked the car and started taking a leisurely stroll through the quaint village of Great Neck looking for a cool spot to grab lunch.

Finally, we nestled into a booth in the back of an empty restaurant, ordered lunch, and the conversation turned to love and relationships. I don't remember all that much about the lunch except that Tony confided that in his then thirty-eight years he'd never been in love. Who spends thirty-eight years on this planet and has never fallen in love? Not even *once*? I thought it was weird and told him so. In fact, I think I harped on the topic a bit to the point where he felt self-conscious about it. But truthfully, I felt sorry for him for never having had the opportunity to make that type of connection with another person. I remembered him telling me during our interview that even Ellen DeGeneres had showed interest in his impaired love life, offering to set him up. But he had always declined. He told me, "I just don't want my love life in public." My interpretation: I don't want to be accountable for my actions. Ok, just my interpretation. Point being, my "player" radar went on – *playdar*.

After lunch, Tony and I emerged from the bistro out onto the street. As we were making our way to my car, a few middle-aged women noticed Tony and they were genuinely excited to see him in their town. One of them said, "That's the guy from the *Ellen* show!" and the group of them began to make their way towards us.

It wasn't me they were interested in, so I simply opened the driver's side door and got into the car, figuring he would do his thing and make their day with some smiles and small talk. Instead, he barely offered a rushed wave as he got into the passenger side of my car, slammed the door shut and said, "Let's get out of here!"

Seriously?!

What was the big friggin' deal about giving a few suburban housewives a thrill and saying "Hello," taking a few pictures and just being pleasant? I didn't agree with the way he handled that encounter, but Tony and I barely knew each other and I didn't feel it was my place to say anything. So we just drove off.

I don't recall how we wound up at my sparsely furnished, just-moved-into apartment, but we were sitting on my sofa, laughing and trading dating war stories, *mostly his*, when he blurted, "See, earlier we weren't really getting along and now look at us."

My memory gets a little foggy until he lunged towards me and went in for the kill. We began making out with my little Shih Ztu, Frankie, hovering over him on the arm of my sofa. I remember thinking to myself,

"I'll make out with you buddy, but that's all you're getting." I had absolutely no intention of taking things further with him that afternoon. Suddenly my dog began really bugging us and constantly trying to get between us as if to say, "Uh-uh, break it up." And then I heard this ditty from Tony, "I guess we won't be getting busy in here." Nope. Guess not.

It's unthinkable to me to have sex with anyone on a first date. Despite some of my previous professional antics, I'm just not that girl. And besides, I was only really moderately interested in him to be honest. It was a sort of "I could take it or leave it" type of scenario.

When it was time to give Tony a ride to the nearest Long Island Railroad station, I changed into my sweats and we made some small talk on the drive to the train station. I don't remember how we said goodbye. I'm sure we exchanged some pleasantries as he got out of the car and told me about his upcoming travel schedule, which included a trip to Europe and then back home to Los Angeles.

Several weeks later I got a wild hair up my ass and texted Tony something like, "Hey" to which he replied, "I'm back in LA." We never spoke again after that.

In 2008, DJ Tony Okungbowa returned *to the Ellen show.*

He left once again in 2013.

CHAPTER NINE

*"I do try to find the happiness and the humor
in life, but that doesn't mean I don't have bad
times. That would make me a robot."*
- told to me by Kristin Chenoweth

I knew my career had picked up traction when,
in April of 2012, publicist Jill Fritzo, whom I had
worked with quite a bit, offered me an interview
with actress, singer and all around acclaimed
performer, Kristin Chenoweth.

I had been working with Jill for quite a while by
this point, having been granted interviews with
some of her other clients like The Kardashians,
Denise Richards, and Tori Spelling, but it didn't
come so easy with Jill. In fact, the first ten or so
interview requests I shot her way weren't even
acknowledged with so much as a "Sorry, but he/she
is not available." I would send an interview request
for her clients and the silence would be deafening.
Knowing I had to get "in" with Jill, I continued to
contact her. If you're in the entertainment business
then you know that at one time Jill Fritzo boasted
a client roster that was a "Who's Who in Popular

Culture." If they were in the celebrity weeklies on a fairly regular basis, there was a good chance that Jill represented them.

I knew that her clients would help me create interview content that would surely have legs in the blogosphere, and I'm nothing if not persistent when I have a goal. One day I was feeling particularly ballsy *(or desperate... or a little of both)* and I sent her an email that went something like this:

Hey Jill,

If you wouldn't mind, can you please give me some idea of what you look for in a media outlet when considering who to grant interviews to for your clients? Getting your feedback would really help us out a lot, and I can assure you that I am not interested in gratuitous or salacious questions that have no journalistic merit. I love to tell someone's true and authentic story to readers. That is my goal. I really don't care who your clients are sleeping with.

Thanks!

Allison

Yes, I really did write that last sentence to her. Whatever I wrote, it must have worked. She warmed up to me a little bit, and after proving my salt by doing a piece on one of her daytime soap opera clients, I landed an interview with Jill's client, Denise Richards. Then I booked interviews with some of her other clients: Tori Spelling, Kim Kardashian, Khloe Kardashian, Meghan Hilty and some others. Then I reeled in a really big fish, at least in my book. One day I looked at my email inbox and there it was.

"Are you interested in talking to Kristin Chenoweth?"

Uh… *yeah.*

Sometimes you have these moments in life where you kind of witness your life as an outside observer looking in; I know I experience this. This was one of those moments. Many times throughout my journalism career, I would think, "How did I get here? Do I really deserve to be here? Who the hell am I?" Then I would take a quick mental inventory of my resume and accomplishments and that would calm me down a bit and put me back into my good head game. It's like a soul suddenly jumping back into its body after an out-of-body experience. When you interview famous people for a living you have a lot of these "outside of myself, witnessing what's going on" moments. I would imagine celebrities have them all the time. Like Charlie Sheen famously said when he accepted a Golden Globe Award in 2002 for his role on *Spin City*. "This is like a sober acid trip."

In addition to exhaustive research, writing my questions, and saying a little prayer that all of my interview questions come from a place of integrity and will be received as such, I try to find common ground with the person I am about to interview. It helps me establish an instant rapport with my interview subject within the first 30 seconds of our chat. It enables things to flow more like an intimate conversation between two friends than a sterile session of questions and answers. In the case of Kristin, my son had been really into *Sesame Street* at the time, and there are some old *Sesame Street* clips of Kristin playing a silly, mime-like character named Ms. Noodle.

"I've been watching you as Ms. Noodle on *Sesame Street* for the longest time because I have a three year old son who just loves the show," I gushed to her. "This morning when I said I was talking to you today, he told me to please say 'Hi' to Ms. Noodle for him."

Kristin promptly and enthusiastically chirped, "Of Course! I'm really big with people under five! You tell him I say hello." Kristin and I then got along famously throughout our entire conversation.

I'll mention this quite a bit throughout this book and some of you might get annoyed or even accuse me of being a kiss up, but I don't care. Because of my spiritual beliefs and studies, when I look at another or engage in a deep conversation with someone, I experience an exchange of energy. I don't just see a person. I see a fellow soul on an eternal journey, no more or less important than my own. That being said, I try to find the value in every exchange, even with those who are more ego-driven personalities.

With Kristin, I really didn't have to search very hard to see her beauty. She has a warmth that emanates from her, and her candor during our interview surprised me a bit. I was impressed by her willingness to share some of the darker sides of herself with me. I mean, we all have them. Nobody can be rainbows and sunshine all the time, not even Kristin Chenoweth.

We began with some of the planned talking points which included her then television series *GCB*, and a new album titled *Some Lessons Learned* for which she would soon be embarking on a North American tour.

At one point in our conversation I paused, and then filled in the silent space with this whopper:

> "… if people were to sum you up, they would likely say, 'God, Kristin Chenoweth, she's so bubbly and full of energy, and happy all the time.' Are you happy most of the time or is that just your default setting when you're in the public eye?"

I fully expected Kristin to protect her bubbly, smiley image by dancing around this question or throwing me something generic, and I would have understood. But she kept it real with me and I respect her so much for that.

Here was part of her answer:

> "There's definitely been times where I've had to put on a happy face even when I didn't feel like it, surely I have. There is a conception about me that I'm happy all the time, I wake up smiling, go to bed smiling, and life is great for me and I have no problems. That's obviously not true because I'm human. I'm also in a very tough business. I have battled depression in my past, and I've been very open about the fact that everything is not perfect, and that nobody's life is. What I have also learned is that people don't want to hear that I would have a problem or a bad day. They think, 'Oh, she's got this great life.' And yes I do and I've been blessed, and I'm thankful. But that doesn't mean that it has been easy and that there have not been times when I wanted to just quit.

> "I've sacrificed to be where I am. I'm sure it is going to come in the years to come, but right now my life is not perfect. Yes, I am a happy person, I am. I do try to find the happiness and the humor in life, but that doesn't mean I don't have bad times. That would make me a robot."

Well put. As I'm sure you can surmise, part of what she was alluding to with me is her single status and not yet being a mom. She let me know that a family of her own is something she does want very badly.

Once she laid that one on me we began to talk a little more freely about how she feels about being single and not yet having children, hard lessons she has endured *(like the rest of us, of course)*, missing her high school reunions due to her hectic work schedule, and the possibility of following in Sandra Bullock's footsteps and adopting a baby one day *(Kristin, herself, is adopted)*.

Here is a quote about Kristin considering adoption, which was picked up by RadarOnline.com and some of the other entertainment news outlets:

> "If I were to have a child, I could see myself adopting a child. I've always kind of not wanted to do it alone. I'd love to have a partner that I could be a parent with, but I look at Sandy Bullock and I think that's a great example. At almost age fifty, she's a mama and she has a baby. I can see that in time I could say, 'I'm going to do that.'"

What I found most interesting about Kristin was that her giddiness is her armor. As we talked about more significant topics together, that branded bubbly exterior was no longer there. I don't mean to say that she suddenly grew dark and brooding on me, but a more genuine fluctuation of emotion came out of her. When she opened up to me about experiencing bouts of depression and having sacrificed having a family up until this point in her life, her voice grew shakier, quieter and more melancholy. It was something I had never seen from her in the media and I suspected it's a part of herself that she generally holds close to the vest. In fact, here is a quote from our interview in which she says as much:

> "The problems and situations that I have will be shared with my closest family members and friends because they are the ones who truly love me, have known me the longest and love me for *me*."

When we spoke about our shared affinity for assisting homeless people and those who are hungry, a raw empathy came through in Kristin. When topics turned to humor, her voice brightened and she giggled, *really* giggled... not because anyone was watching, but because she was happy, and very excited to be performing for friends and family back in her hometown of Broken Arrow, Oklahoma on her North American tour.

My interview with Kristin Chenoweth generated a lot of sound bite media pick-ups from all of the ABC, NBC, CBS and FOX news affiliate websites throughout the country; on RadarOnline.com,

PopCultureMadness.com, on her official fan site and through W.E.N.N. syndication (World Entertainment News Network).

Perhaps my favorite media pick up of all was on Kristin's own Twitter feed. It read:

"@PRcomArticles I thought she really got me."

Deep in thought in Delray Beach, Florida.

CHAPTER TEN

*"The earth itself will keep spinning, but people
won't even be here if women aren't given a
greater hold over the social process."
- told to me by Russell Simmons*

In the early days, picking up the phone to ask for an interview always turned my stomach to knots. Let me re-state: I flat-out hated doing it. Of course my skin thickened soon enough, and after a couple of years it was as routine for me as dialing up Domino's Pizza. But I was still pretty green one morning in 2005 when I dialed up the publicity office for Hip Hop impresario and cultural icon, Russell Simmons. I was requesting an interview to be published on our fledgling online publication, PR.com. I already had a modest handful of notable interviews under my belt, but on this day my budding journalism resume did little to calm my nerves.

"Russell Simmons's office?" the already impatient voice spat out. "Hi, my name is Allison Kugel. I'm calling from the website PR.com to request an interview with Mr. Simmons to appear on our…"

"I'm sorry, *where* are you calling from?" the voice interrupted in a curt tone. "Uh, PR.com. We're an online newswire and I'm calling to request an interview with Russell Simmons."

There was a silent pause that dropped in the air. "I'm sorry. I've never heard of you and Russell has more important things to do than to speak to you. You're wasting my time." Click. Dial tone.

Ok, before I continue on, yes, this really did happen. No, I am not taking any creative license, and I will mercifully not disclose that publicist's name. I'm actually embarrassed for her, and if I ever caught anyone who worked for me speaking to someone that way they would be fired on the spot. I don't care if it's the president of the United States or the company janitor. No one who works for me would ever be allowed to speak to another human being in that way. It's not a reflection on Russell Simmons at all. I am sure he would take the same attitude as me, had he witnessed what happened.

I slowly clicked the button to hang up the phone on my end and gazed blankly for an un-quantified amount of time before that heavy feeling of failure crept in and began to circulate through my veins. I immediately picked up the phone to call my editor, Jason, in hopes of recounting the story in a playful manner. I figured a good laugh would soothe my utterly deflated mood.

As I recounted that unpleasant phone conversation to him, he gave me the typical pep talk that I assumed I would get, but as many perfectionists do, I play devil's advocate ad nauseam. I repeatedly argue my case of hopelessness until the other party folds out of frustration. Exasperated with my seeming theatrics, he finally declared my argument valid just to get me to stop arguing. I insisted that I was never going to get someone as widely celebrated as Russell Simmons, or any major celebrity for that matter, to sit down for an interview with me. Who was *I*? Just some girl with a dream of interviewing not some, but all, of the most influential newsmakers of our time. One by one, I dreamt, I would knock them out of the park and I would eventually amass a humongous online journal of Q & A conversations with various famous people. My journalistic diary-of-sorts would then be read by people the world over, and someday I would turn those conversations and the stories behind them into a book.

But on that cold day more than a decade ago as winter stubbornly persevered, with the phone still staring me squarely in the eye, I felt I would never reach my goals. I was certain that whomever that woman was on the other end of the phone line, she must have sensed that I was not worthy and felt it was her duty to put me in my place and tell me so. We've all had those moments, haven't we? Whether it was a school bully, a romantic rejection or losing out on a job, we then let that experience sink its hooks into us. I am now better able to take these experiences with a grain of salt, and when I feel myself getting into a funk I'll joke with a friend about how I'm "having a moment." My closest friends and I provide each other with a built-in fan base. We like to remind each other of how kick ass we know we really are. It works.

The day was December 9, 2010, and at 11 AM EST I was scheduled to be connected to Russell Simmons for our one-on-one interview to discuss the evolution of his lifestyle brand. That discouraging day back in 2005 was the furthest thing from my mind as I feverishly prepared my notes of research gathered in the wee hours of the morning; at 3 AM to be exact. I then patiently awaited Mr. Simmons' phone call while multitasking other projects that were in the works. My interview credits had grown substantially by now, and things were a matter of routine at this point.

The phone rang right on time, and it was Mr. Simmons' assistant, Adair Curtis, on the line. Adair is a kind and accommodating man who told me he would promptly connect me to Mr. Simmons for our interview.

When the conversation began, Russell said, "So what are we talking about today?" I said, "Well, I know we need to focus on your new clothing line, Argyle Culture."

Russell wanted to take things in a slightly different direction. "What about the book? You didn't get the book?" he asked with urgency.

"No, no one sent me your book! We can talk about it though, and then after I read it I'll edit everything together," I offered. I froze for a second, wondering how I would cover a book I had never read or even seen any notes on.

Russell summoned Adair to arrange to have a copy of his latest literary effort, *Super Rich: A Guide To Having It All*, shipped out to me ASAP. After asking Russell about the basic principles of his book, I thanked God that I had the foresight to thoroughly study Russell's spiritual beliefs inside and out, backwards and forwards. We steered our ship in that direction for much of the interview.

At the risk of sounding "kind of out there" to many of you, I've been studying matters of spirituality and the eternal journey of the soul for nearly a decade now. I am right at home swimming in those waters and I can hold my own in most conversations pertaining to this subject. *Super Rich* mainly covered the process of approaching prosperity from the inside out, dealing first with the self and what you project out to the world, with financial prosperity manifesting as a result of spiritual balance and inner wealth and well-being.

Here is a passage from my interview with Russell that talks about his devotion to the practice of Yoga and his methods of prayer:

> Russell Simmons: I'm a yogi. Yoga scripture was written long before there was ever Buddhist scripture, or before there was the Bible or Koran or a Torah. Yoga sutras are science for happiness. My religion is compassion. Yoga sutras are a science that I practice daily, and religiously. Classic yoga has eight steps and there are social laws. The first steps are the Damas and they are like social laws, they are like the Ten Commandments and they were written and past on years before [religion]. Science of yoga, science for happiness is the same basis that exists in all scripture written before most modern-day religious practices. And it mirrors what is in all religion. I do wear Buddha images, but the Buddha scripture is mostly taken from the yoga sutras.

> **Allison Kugel: When you pray, who do you pray to, or *what* do you pray to?**

> Russell Simmons: I pray to Atman, to the self. The Atman is self. If God were the ocean, you would be a piece of the God. In other words, you would be connected to the animals, to the planet and to everybody. When you practice compassion, you practice compassion to all

of these things because all of these things are you, and you are them. That is a way that some yogis, Christian yogis, would view it; Christian yogis like Paramahansa Yogananda who believed in Christ as a miracle worker, but also believed in all of the prophets.

Aside from the clarity that emanates from Russell Simmons when you speak with him, I was impressed to find him to be a staunch feminist. It's not that every man has to beat the feminism drums to make me happy, quite the contrary. I don't mind men being men and women being women, just so long as there is equal and mutual respect. But I took note of Russell's slant on gender equality, mostly because it's quite an anomaly within the hip hop community which was his origin. In hip hop and urban culture, misogynistic song lyrics and behaviors can run rampant at times. I asked him about some of the anti-female lyrics and attitudes within hip hop, and here is what he had to say:

Allison Kugel: What are your thoughts on some of the rougher lyrics that continue to tear down the young urban female rather than building her up?

Russell Simmons: Ugh! What are my thoughts about the preacher who won't let the woman in the pulpit or the firemen who are just completely sexist, and their kids hear it all day and it rubs off on them, or the previous generation's sexism? My thoughts about sexism, in general is that it's horrible. My feeling about women's rights is that they should have equal rights, and they just got equal pay yesterday from the President. Abuse of women and a lack of [female] input in society today is why we have the wars and the abuse of animals and the abuse of each other that we have. Women's input, and not women who take on this hardened element, but the female side of the brain and the female physical being is being separated from the decision making process, and it is the reason that the Earth is spinning off its axis. Or, actually, the people will spin off the axis. The Earth itself will keep spinning, but people won't even be here if women aren't given a greater hold over the social process. They will make choices that really embody compassion and love in the way that they are able to give it.

Allison Kugel: I have posed that question to many different people in your industry and have never gotten an answer like that before. What I usually get is a defensive answer.

Russell Simmons: Women are abused. Women have been locked out of everything throughout history, and even in religion. Religion has undermined women.

Allison Kugel: I always felt good about myself and never felt I was anything less than equal, but after I gave birth I felt like a force to be reckoned with.

Russell Simmons: Yeah, but you are still less than equal, believe me. Just like black people still are. They are all poor, aren't they? Aren't black people still poor all over the world?

Allison Kugel: You're certainly not poor.

Russell Simmons: Black people, the collective. Not me. A woman might [someday] be President and Hillary Clinton is Secretary of State and there was never a chance that she wouldn't be the same price as a man, but women in general, black people in general, all over the world are poor. Women all over the world are less than human and less than equal. Even in religion they've been…

Allison Kugel: Under the thumb of men.

Russell Simmons: That's a good way of putting it, yeah. But women in hip hop, they speak out about it much more than women in other forms of cultural phenomenon; they really do speak out. They talk about being equal and better than equal in a way that is very convincing.

Russell Simmons and I spoke for about forty minutes and the conversation left a distinct impression on me. He is a spiritual man who clearly has a lot to say about everything from gender and racial equality to animal rights, to the benefits of devoting oneself to the practice of yoga.

Finally, we did come around to talking about Russell's new apparel line, Argyle Culture, but the subject matter felt like an organic extension in the evolution of our conversation. And of course, our dialogue went well beyond fashion. We made it more philosophical; even political.

> ***Allison Kugel: What was your evolution as a designer, going from the Phat Farm label to Argyle Culture?***

> Russell Simmons: It was honest. For the last four or five years with Phat Farm I had trouble designing clothes that fit into the department where I was shipping, the young men's department. Now I'm designing for the men's department and I am having a lot more fun and it is more honest. It's honest evolution and honest distribution. I'm a man, I make men's clothes. Adam Sandler grew up on Phat Farm and he is still wearing it, and I'm sending him Argyle Culture. The President grew up on Phat Farm and he is now wearing Polo like every other man who grew up on Phat Farm.

It is something that didn't really represent his generation, and we are trying now to serve this urban graduate.

Allison Kugel: What I got from the Argyle Culture line, and I could be going too deep, but what I got from it is that it speaks to more opportunities, more education and more self-esteem, hence a more sophisticated look.

Russell Simmons: All of that can come from it, but the truth is that it speaks to more maturity and, yes, it does have to do with more success.

Allison Kugel: And more opportunities in the 21st century.

Russell Simmons: People who had their pants hanging off their ass, now suddenly they're joining the mainstream.

Allison Kugel: (Laughs.) It's really amazing that the political landscape trickles down to everything from our films, music, fashion and so many other things. The fact that President Obama is in office, I feel that might have unconsciously had an effect on where you wanted to take your product line.

Russell Simmons: All things lead to the next generation and what hip hop graduates are, urban graduates I call them.

Allison Kugel: How are men embracing this new clothing line?

Russell Simmons: It's selling very well. All of the small sizes are sold out. I think that some of the buyers thought it was all the same audience and that they were all bigger sizes and hip hop [style], and they found out that it was not a "black line," and not oversized. They found that all of the sizes that people wanted sold out the minute it hit the store and they can buy it correctly just like they buy Lacoste or any other men's line.

Allison Kugel: The pants hanging off the ass was kind of a "f*ck you" to a society that was un- accepting and exclusionary, and now this new way of dressing speaks to a feeling of, "I can be a part of the mainstream and succeed."

Russell Simmons: Very good. I wish I had said that.

Anytime someone I interviewed made a point to tell me that they like or appreciate the way I phrased something or told me that they felt touched or inspired by something I told them, my insides would smile with sheer giddiness. It's those moments that were always confirmation for me that I was exactly where I should be, doing exactly what I should be doing. As author Gary Zukav would describe it, it let me know that my little tugboat was indeed following the great mother ship that is my soul. Here's how Gary puts it:

> "As you follow your inner sense of meaning, you are sailing in the same direction your mothership wants to sail." – *Gary Zukav*

Love that.

Beyond the intellectually stimulating company of Mr. Simmons, I distinctly felt an inner nudge that told me my professional efforts had somehow come full circle, but I had no conscious memory of why at that particular moment.

My favorite part about this job was that an interview can take on a life of its own and you can end up at a completely different destination than you anticipated, going in. When I booked this interview with Russell's team, I thought that the focus would be on his *(then)* newest line of apparel. I don't mean to say that I thought that is all we would be discussing, but I thought that would be the promotional anchor of the interview.

When I was connected to Russell and we introduced ourselves he was excited to talk about his latest book, *Super Rich*, of which no one had so much as mentioned to me, prior.

In that moment as I hung up the phone this time, I felt accomplished and privileged to be able to have this private front row seat with so many remarkable people who are continually shaping our world. Moreover, this was a seat that I created. No one gave it to me or reserved it for me, I built that chair for myself.

As I was walking over to my boyfriend to recap my day's events as we always would do in the evening, December of 2005 re-appeared in my memory. It was as if an assistant was thumbing through my mental files, stumbled upon that demoralizing day, dusted off the file and opened it up for me. I suddenly remembered my first go around at trying to book Mr. Simmons for an interview. A smirk spread across my face.

This was a great lesson for me. Sometimes we get so caught up in a disappointing or discouraging moment that we lose sight of the bigger picture. I really try not to do that these days if I can help it.

I did read Russell's book, *Super Rich*... after I interviewed him. Yet thanks to my seamless editing techniques no one was the wiser. But the book makes some good points about how we tend to live our lives backwards, in a sense.

CHAPTER ELEVEN

"Just write 'Happy Birthday, Love Allison.'"
- told to me by Dave Chappelle

My first foray into the entertainment industry was after my sophomore year of college when I landed an internship in New York City working for a talent management company. This particular company represented and managed the careers of some of today's most successful comics. Back then they were all either unknowns or almost-but-not-quite famous, and working hard to make a name for themselves. People like Wanda Sykes, Jim Breuer, Daryl Hammond, Jeff Ross and the now somewhat infamous, yet legendary, Dave Chappelle. As I mentioned earlier, I had grown quite fond of comedy as a medicinal balm during some of my rougher adolescent years. The appreciation for great comedy stuck with me.

In addition to Murphy, Pryor and Williams, along with other geniuses like George Carlin, The Three Stooges, Jackie Gleason's portrayal of Ralph

Cramden in *The Honeymooners*, Carol O'Conner's portrayal of Archie Bunker in *All in the Family*, I was impressed with the way comedy could deliver an important message while simultaneously lifting my spirits. These brilliant artists still make me split my sides with laughter. So I knew I was in for an interesting summer of fun and learning when I went to work for Barry Katz Management and New York Entertainment in the summer of 1994. Shortly before I began working at their office, Barry and one of his then-employees, Jason Steinberg, had discovered a young comedian from Washington, DC, named Dave Chappelle. They spotted him performing at the comedy club Barry owned at the time. It was called The Boston Comedy Club and was located in the heart of Manhattan's West Village.

The Boston Comedy Club was a small, dimly lit room located on W 3rd Street, with booths lining the back wall and some small bistro style tables scattered throughout the floor leading up to a small stage. From what I heard plenty of times from Jason Steinberg, one night an unknown comic named Dave Chappelle, who couldn't have been more than eighteen at the time, wandered into the club and performed a set. Jason was so struck by his stage presence and charisma that he promptly brought Dave to the attention of his boss Barry Katz, who signed him on the spot. That's the abridged version, anyway. In fact, there was lingering tension among the ranks as to who the actual visionary was who officially discovered Dave; Jason or Barry?

By the summer of 1994 I was a nineteen year old college student and Dave was a twenty-one year old steadily working comic with film and television credits, and headlining gigs across the country. He was also prepping and tightening his set to make his first appearance on *Late Show with David Letterman*. Anyone familiar with the business knows that comics tend to be night owls and they usually have their days free to do with as they please, or to take meetings around town. The comedy scene was booming around that time and Barry and Jason were always working a mile a minute to get their roster of clients booked on *Comedy Central*, on the late night talk shows and television network development deals. The brass ring was thought to be a network development deal for a sitcom pilot, or for an HBO special.

At the time, Dave was on this same trajectory. At least a couple of times a week he and a friend of his who worked at The Boston Comedy Club would drop by the office to get in some facetime with the agents and to just hang out. Sometimes Dave and I would find ourselves alone in one of the agent's offices with nothing to do but shoot the shit about dating, relationships or gossip about common acquaintances. I was a college student and he was a working professional but we were essentially both kids. He'd confide in me about various girls he was interested in and I would tell him about the guys around campus I had dated the previous semester. On one particular day Dave had a sensitive bit of information regarding a mutual friend who had cheated on his girlfriend, so he called me out to the balcony off the main offices so we could talk in private. People could see us whispering closely through the window. We must have been out there for a while, because when he and I walked back inside we got some sideways looks.

Next thing I knew I was fending off rumors of a new couple alert. That couldn't have been further from the truth; in fact, we seemed to have developed more of a brother/sister type of vibe.

In 1995, when I returned to school after that momentous summer internship, I took over my campus's position as chairperson of comedy bookings. In short order I booked Jeff Ross as an opening act, with Dave appearing as the headliner of the evening. I even got an inside deal on both Jeff and Dave's price quotes which our budget was very grateful for. The show sold out and was standing room only. Throughout Dave's set he continued to tease and jibe me as I tried to give him silent signals from off stage as to how long his set was and when to wrap it up so I could close the show. I should have known there was no way he was going to take direction from me, but I didn't mind as it was all in good fun.

Our friendship continued, with me visiting The Boston Comedy Club as a regular. Every time I would bring one of my girlfriends down to The

Boston Comedy club at night to catch a show, Dave would fall head over heels and ask if she was single. Every. Time. It would typically go something like this.

"Dave, this is Sara. Sara, Dave."

Halfway into the evening, Dave would pull me aside.

"Oh my God, she's so adorable and sweet. I don't know if I wanna fuck her or hug her. Do you think she would go out with me?"

"She has a boyfriend."

A few weeks later…

"Dave, this is Lisa. Lisa, Dave."

Halfway into the evening, Dave pulled me aside.

"Is it ok if I ask out your friend? Do you think she would go out with me? I want to take her to go see *Jerry Maguire*."

"She actually has a boyfriend."

I wasn't bullshitting. For some reason all of my friends had boyfriends around that time. Although about a year later, Lisa and Dave did mess around a little in the back of a limo, and right in front of me.

It was now late 1998 or early 1999. My former boss Jason Steinberg was throwing a big blowout bash, though I can't remember the occasion. I had been living in Los Angeles by now and flew in to New York to visit with family and to attend the party. Dave showed up and I was there with Lisa as my guest. Lisa was on the outs with her boyfriend over some argument that had just taken place, and she was feeling flirtatious that night. We were all hanging out in a group just having the best time. When Lisa and I were ready to head out Dave asked us for a ride back to his place, downtown. I happened to have had a stretch limo on call for us that night, roughly the size of a small apartment inside. I mean, this thing was so humongous, I thought the back might detach from the driver's cab on some of the sharper turns into the city.

When we were all ready to leave the party, I hopped into the back of the car followed by Lisa, and finally Dave. The two of them sat oddly close to one another and Lisa began dropping hints like crazy; maybe it was the alcohol. We were about 4 or 5 blocks from pulling up to Dave's building when she suddenly lunged at him, throwing him onto the floor of the limo and jumping on top of him. They began making out and groping at each other. Not knowing what else to do, I simply starred straight at them for what felt like forever until the car came to a sudden stop. The driver abruptly opened the door to find the two of them that way. It was awkward as ass, so I screamed, "Shut the door, will ya!" The driver shut the door and waited outside for those two to collect themselves.

Dave stumbled to his feet smirking and feigning bewilderment. He uttered, "Call me," in a high pitched, mockingly sheepish tone at Lisa as he exited the car.

"What was that all about?" I probed at Lisa. "Now I have a story to tell my kids one day," she casually offered with a shrug. A few months later she married her boyfriend.

Only a few days after that, uh, interesting night in New York, I was coming out of the Beverly Center shopping mall in Los Angeles and waiting at the valet stand when I felt a body come up behind me and press two hands firmly over my eyes. I was ready to freak out when I heard a familiar voice say, "Guess who?!" I spun around and it was Dave Chappelle. We hugged as I said, "Fancy seeing you here!" with a laugh.

He explained that he had just flown out to shoot a television pilot and the network he was working for was putting him up at the Hotel Nikko on La Cienega Blvd. near Beverly Hills *(it has long since been bought over by Le Meridien)*. We decided to hang out and grab some lunch later that day and I agreed to meet him at his hotel room at the Nikko.

My *Playboy's College Girls* issue had recently hit newsstands and he didn't miss the opportunity to tease me about it, saying, "Oh, and could you bring me a copy of your *Playboy* issue and some lotion when you come here?"

I recoiled as I retorted, "Eww, you perv." He then back peddled and claimed he legitimately forgot to pack lotion. *Errr.*

An hour later I showed up at his hotel room with a copy of my *Playboy* issue in one hand and a bottle of Moisturel lotion in the other, not knowing what to think. I put them down and we both laughed. He then said, "But, seriously, can you please autograph it for me?"

"You want me to autograph this magazine for you?" I shot back sarcastically. "Yea. Funny. Now I know how people feel when they ask me for *my* autograph," he mused.

"Dave, I don't know what the hell to write. It's so awkward."

He scrunched his face for a second and then offered, "Just write 'Dear Dave, Happy Birthday. Love, Allison.'"

"Is it your birthday?" I asked him. "No," he playfully shot back. "But it's just something to write."

I took the magazine in my hands, flipped it open to my six picture pictorial as my face flushed a beat red shade and felt hot with embarrassment. I scribbled as fast as I could, "Happy Birthday, Love Allison."

I then ordered him to take that bottle of lotion and get it out of site immediately before I kicked his ass.

We hopped in his rented Lexus sedan and headed out for lunch with Janet Jackson's *Velvet Rope* CD playing in the car. As Dave puffed on a cigarette he expressed his frustration to me about the contract he was locked into with a certain television network which entitled them to keep making him do pilot after pilot until his contract ran out. He explained that it was keeping him from being able to audition for or accept roles in feature films and he was resentful about it. *Half Baked*, a movie Dave had co-written and starred in with comedian Jim Breuer had hit theaters the previous year and found a cult following. But it was virtually eclipsed by James Cameron's mega-release, *Titanic*. "That damn ship!" Dave screamed jokingly when discussing the timing of the release of *Half Baked*.

"I wanna make 'fuck you' money. Do you know what 'fuck you' money is?" he turned to me and asked. I didn't. From where I was sitting he seemed to have it all. Who wouldn't want a network deal and the opportunity to keep shooting TV pilots, I thought. I saw a guy with a pretty good set up as far as I was concerned, so I didn't quite get it at the time. Though

I will admit, we were existing in two different worlds. I was just getting my life going at that time, and he was headlong into the world of dealing with corporate red tape and politics. I get it now.

It was around this time, as 1998 rolled into 1999 that I went from managing my anxiety with some simple deep breathing exercises to people pushing Prozac at me from every corner. I felt like Tony Soprano in the first season of *The Sopranos* when Dr. Melfi tells Tony, "With today's pharmacology, no one needs to suffer with feelings of exhaustion and depression." Tony skeptically responds to Dr. Melfi with, "Here we go. Here comes the Prozac." Indeed. Here comes the Prozac.

Here's how it went down.

By my early twenties I was an old pro at dealing with intermittent bouts of anxiety and panic attacks. It was basically my normal. Like someone who lives with migraines, stomach issues, allergies. We all have something. Well, this was my something. Other than sometimes being a bit more highly strung and a little bit more sensitive than the average bear, life rolled along. For the most part it didn't get in my way... unless it did.

Since I was living a somewhat bicoastal life at the time, I saw no issue with dating someone who lived in New York even though I was based in LA most of the time. There was this handsome Italian guy I had seen when our paths crossed at a modeling agency in New York shortly before my move out west. I don't remember the particulars of that encounter, but we ended up exchanging phone numbers and we went on a date shortly before my big move, in January of 1998. It struck me on our first date that he was good looking, charismatic and appeared to have a lot going for him, and yet seemed to have pretty low self-esteem. Strange dichotomy. He was a law student living in a tony area on the north shore of Long Island with his grandparents. I do recall him telling me that his mother was not exactly parent material and so his grandparents stepped up to the plate to raise him. The mom issues, and a lot of other things I picked up on should have been a major red flag, but I liked him. Aside from disturbing family strife, I also came to find out that he suffered from a mild form of Turrets' Syndrome. It gave him a slight tic that I guess was just bothersome enough to create some deep insecurities.

We kept in touch when I was in LA and when I made trips home to New York we dated. On one such trip I kept extending my stay in New York because we were getting pretty close and I didn't feel like leaving. But after three weeks I had business to attend to in LA and I had to fly back. Well, a couple of weeks after that trip I was dumped over the phone pretty unceremoniously. I chalked it up to being for the best since we lived on opposite coasts and there were always things that kind of nagged at me about him that I couldn't quite shake. A few weeks later, just as I was putting this guy in my rear view mirror the phone rang and it was him, begging for a second chance. His pleas struck me as strange only because we hadn't been together that long, hadn't said "I love you" or anything like that. And being the character I can sometimes be once someone crosses me, I sarcastically deadpanned, "Ok. You have five minutes. Let's hear your pitch."

What came out of his mouth next was startling and shook me to my core. I sat upright in my bed in Los Angeles as he made some serious confessions from his home in New York. I stress the geographical distance in this sentence because had we been in the same city I don't know what I would have done. I'm glad there were 3,000 miles between us during that call. He began rambling about me inspiring him to want to be a better man and how he had been living a rather dark and risky existence for years and was ready to reform. I felt bad for him and countered his statements by assuring him nothing could be that bad as he was insinuating. Before I could finish, he cut me off and blurted out a confession about a long term prostitute addiction that had dated back to college and had still been ongoing while he and I were dating. As he made his confessions about his lifestyle and cleared his own conscience with each statement, I began to feel cold shivers running up and down my spine. My heart started pounding and I felt this sensation of imminent dread wash over me. You have to remember that the nineties was ground zero for all things HIV and AIDS awareness. Everyone in the nineties was paranoid about HIV and AIDS, clinging to condoms the way they clung to lifeboats during the sinking of the Titanic. It was a nerve wracking time to be single.

In an instant I felt paralyzed, violated, terrified, betrayed. I had made a choice to be intimate with this person on several occasions without the benefit of having all of the facts at my disposal, and that sickened me. This person who had a prostitute habit had put me in harm's way, I thought. And yes I used protection, but the fact remained, I was put in a compromising position. I had been with a high risk partner without knowing it. As I mentioned earlier, people with anxiety and panic all have their own unique triggers. Mine happened to be any threat of physical harm or illness. That's my trigger and the triggers were going off like gangbusters that horrible night. I tried to remain composed so I could ask *and re-ask* him as many questions as I could think of. I was trying to convince myself I was not in danger, but nothing worked. I was a goner… emotionally, anyway. The worst part was that I knew I would have to wait three months to get tested and then wait an additional three months to get re-tested. In that moment I felt so helpless. This may seem strange to some but my first instinct after that horrific phone call was to call my parents and confess every detail. At the end of the day my family are my best friends. When the shit really hits the fan, they are who I run to.

For weeks after that night, I was in a constant state of anxiety and terror: calling doctors, clinics, friends, anyone who I thought might be able to provide me with some piece of mind; some magic answer that would set my mind at ease. Finally, I managed to dump my exhausted, strung out body onto a flight bound for New York, where I hid out at my parents' house. I was in an unrecognizable state: thin, drawn, in a fog and vulnerable. Intermittently, I would go on these crying jags, beating myself up for not having better judgement in who I had chosen to be with and trust.

I even bought a pack of condoms and began pushing my hand into them, trying my hardest to cause them to break, and I would retrace my steps in my mind, trying desperately to remember if every condom I had used had remained intact or if there were any times I had been less then completely careful. I was in an obsessive, compulsive anxious tailspin and finally my parents dragged me to a psychologist for emergency help.

The psychologist I went to was a man by the name of Gerard Bomse, a brilliant psychologist whom I would seek counseling from on and off until his death in 2010. He changed my life in so many ways and I am forever grateful for his wisdom and help. But in that moment of acute crisis, as my father was shuttling me to Dr. Bomse's office every other day, he finally looked me square in the eye and said, "Listen, Allison. Don't be a hero. Please take some help in the form of medicine."

Everyone who knows me, knows that I despise drugs of any kind. I don't drink, don't smoke weed, and have never, ever even seen hard drugs up close. I also don't like over-the-counter meds. I just don't like drugs. So it was a hard sell to get me to acquiesce to taking something during this crazy time. But the fact of the matter was, I wasn't functioning. I was the walking dead. My parents, my shrink and even a psychiatrist got in on the act to try to convince me to please take some medication to help balance things out. This is when I was introduced to the world of SSRI (selective serotonin reuptake inhibitor) drugs. Prozac was the first breakout star of this classification of drugs, so it was the first one they tried on me. I surrendered and began taking a small dose of Prozac because I knew something had to give, and I had to get back to my life. Between the therapy, family support and a little medication, I was able to get back on my feet and get back to my life in Los Angeles. Eventually three months came and went and I tested negative for HIV and all STDs. I actually made a practice of getting myself tested every year after that point.

Life began to come back together but as the weeks and months went on people around me started to notice something strange in my behavior. I was brimming with manic energy, becoming a bit arrogant and somewhat hyperactive. I was not myself. I felt almost, high. I knew something was a bit left of center but I was actually enjoying the ultra-happy, ultra-energetic new and improved me. But then it began to take a strange turn and I became agitated and antagonistic. Something wasn't right. I went to my local doctor in Santa Monica and said, "This is going to sound weird, but I think the Prozac is having a narcotic effect on me. I mean, I feel high." We tried taking me off of the Prozac, and as the days and weeks went on I began to feel like someone had taken the batteries out of my back. I was like an old toy winding down in power. I was feeling slow and depressed. Eventually I was put on a very small dose of Paxil, which I remain on to this day. There has been much debate about the benefits and risks of SSRI medications. People argue their validity and I have heard my fair share of comments over the years about how I should try to get off of my medication. I have to say I take offense to those kinds of statements. No one has done more research on anxiety and available treatments than I have. No one has studied more, talked to more people and weighed the facts more than me. An interesting fun fact that arose back in 2009 during my pregnancy with my son, was that it was discovered that I had lower than normal levels of serotonin in my blood during some routine blood work to check my platelet count. You wouldn't shame a diabetic for taking insulin and you wouldn't shame someone for taking Synthroid for a thyroid condition. Why should people be shamed for taking medication to balance out their body's brain chemistry? To keep it simple, the hormone Serotonin is a happy chemical our brains produce that keeps our moods stabilized. Your brain releases some serotonin and after your brain has reaped some nice benefits from it, it gets reabsorbed into your body. Some people either don't secrete enough, or what they do secrete gets reabsorbed a little bit too quickly before your brain gets to enjoy it. SSRI medications like Prozac, Paxil, Lexapro, Zoloft, and the like, keep the helpful serotonin from being reabsorbed too fast, so you always have a nice flow of it in your brain. According to MayoClinic.org, "SSRIs block the reabsorption (reuptake) of the neurotransmitter serotonin in the brain. Changing the balance of serotonin seems to help brain cells send and receive chemical messages, which in turn boosts mood."

I have learned many tricks of the trade over the years. Deep breathing, meditation, long walks, a balanced diet, lots of love and laughter, and, yes, talk therapy when I feel I need it to get me through a rough patch. There are many tools in my toolbox. Paxil just happens to be one of them.

In a strange twist of fate, in 2008 I ran into the guy responsible for causing that 1999 anxiety tailspin with his scandalous sexual confessions. So much time had passed and the universe knows exactly when to place people in our path to create catharsis. Everything is always right on time. I was now happily in my relationship with my son's father, Patrick, elated to be 3 months pregnant, and in a great place in my life when we ran into each other and began a casual conversation to catch up. Our short lived relationship wasn't brought up, nor was the explosive and fear-inducing way it had ended. It just didn't matter anymore.

In 2005, I had just moved back east for good, settled into an Upper East Side apartment and began enjoying New York life once again. My family has held season tickets to the Knicks for years, only four rows off the floor and right behind the home basket. Our Knicks games are ritualistic at this point. In the fall of 2005 I was sitting courtside *(well, almost courtside)* with my family catching a game when my mom and brother pointed to the VIP section down below and said, "Hey, isn't that Dave sitting there?" They were referring to Dave Chappelle who I hadn't spoken to in several years. We had lost touch. I fixed my eyes on where they were pointing and spotted him. Even from where I was sitting I could tell that something about his demeanor was different. I got up from my seat, made my way down to the floor seats right in front of him and gave him a playful rub on the head. He looked up, with minimal energy, looking a little out of it, and said, "Hey. I thought you were living in LA." I told him I had moved back to New York and asked how he was doing. *Chappelle's Show* was taking Comedy Central by storm and Dave had become a Generation Y folk hero. He was supposedly the man of the moment, but he didn't seem like it up close.

He didn't have that same playful, joyous energy he had always seemed to carry and he appeared a bit dazed and out of it. He just seemed… off. We made some small talk and I told him it was good to see him. The game had started back up again so I made my way back to my seat. My brother asked me how Dave was doing and I said, "I don't know. He seemed a little out of it. It was weird."

I can then remember some announcement being made that Dave needed to make his way to the men's room and that security had to be put in place as he walked through the crowd at Madison Square Garden so that he wouldn't be mobbed on his way from the stadium to the bathroom. I don't believe that the "fuck you money" or his brief and extreme fling with that kind of rabid fame really made him happy at all.

In the end, I believe it was him and his microphone on a stage, like back in those earlier days at The Boston Comedy Club that truly did and does feed his soul.

CHAPTER TWELVE

*"It does take an enormous amount of strength,
courage and resources for women to win, and
we work to make that happen."*
- told to me by Gloria Allred

Ambulance chaser, femi-nazi, media whore, angry… Attorney Gloria Allred has heard it all said about her, and then some. She is a strong woman with a thick skin, and a confidence in who she is and what she cares about. She recognizes the fear and misconception that often precedes the insults thrown her way and sloughs them off in the interest of fighting the good fight.

How do I know this about her character? I had the pleasure of spending several hours with her. We sat together in a New York hotel room as we filmed an on-camera interview shortly after the Tiger Woods/ Rachel Uchitel madness broke out in the New York media.

It was January of 2010 and Gloria Allred was in the news, yet again. She had scheduled and then canceled a press conference where her client, Tiger

Woods' alleged mistress, Rachel Uchitel was all set to tell what was expected to be her side of the story in the Tiger Woods cheating scandal that had gossip media transfixed and hungry for every detail. When the press conference was abruptly cancelled by Allred in the eleventh hour, legal analysts, and media alike, assumed that Uchitel had been paid off to keep quiet. Some speculated the sum to be as high as $10 million. When I sat down across from Allred and asked her about her most recent client, I was hit with the dreaded "no comment" more times than I would have liked.

The morning of the interview with Gloria was a bit of a mixed bag. My son was eight months old at this time, and his father Patrick and I were having some problems in our relationship. There were good months, so-so months, and bad months, but I was resolute in holding our family together. My own happiness wasn't so much of an issue at this point; our son's happiness was at center stage for me. It takes two to maintain a healthy relationship and two to cause it to unravel, I will admit, but much of the current strife centered on an unfortunate yet all too common problem: alcoholism. Now, six years later, Patrick is the first to admit that he had battled alcoholism and is now in recovery. These days I am very proud of his progress as a human being and a wonderful father. However, 2010 to 2012, in retrospect, was the eye of the storm with this insidious disease.

Patrick is one of the kindest, most gentle souls I have ever known; a truly great person with a huge heart. His alcoholism never translated to violence or moods swings around the house or drinking in front of our son or any of the stereotypical tell-tale signs that would make my alarm bells go off. Being an almost lifelong teetotaler myself, I must admit that I was pretty clueless about drinking, in general. Patrick's alcoholism was closeted and kind of intermittent, so it was confusing and hard to pin down. Frankly, I think it even confused him and enabled some denial.

No, this alcoholism would rear its head whenever there was some stress either pertaining to a family matter or a financial matter. Patrick would give me some song and dance about wanting to go out for a couple of hours to meet up with friends for dinner and maybe a game of pool; guy's night out kind of stuff. It would usually be sprung on me at the last moment and before I knew it he would be out the door with promises of returning home at a respectable hour, like 10 or 11 PM the latest. At one point these nights out were becoming a bit more frequent. I felt they were inappropriate because we had a baby at home and I was exhausted between work and motherhood. Also, while he was letting off steam with his friends, I was feeling broken hearted wondering why he wasn't seeking solace and relaxation in spending time together as a couple once our son went down for sleep. All in all, it wasn't the best dynamic, but I was largely in the dark about the role that alcohol played in this pattern. I could recall a handful or sporadic nights sprinkled throughout our relationship when he would go missing for something like 24 hours or more and I would be frantically trying to track him down, hoping against hope that he was alive as I dialed his parents, my parents, his siblings, his closest friends, looking for some clues.

The end result was, he would either stumble in at 5 or 6 in the morning with a story of passing out somewhere or a friend would call me up in the wee hours of the morning explaining that he had too much to drink and was passed out on their couch. This would be followed by them pleading with me to go easy on him when he returned home the following day. One such night when I was nine months pregnant, I was incensed to receive a call at 3:30 AM from some girl I didn't know well *(but who had a bad reputation)*, explaining that he had partied too hard and was sleeping it off on her couch. Needless to say, there was a fight that next day. The charm was wearing thin, to put it mildly. Another time, I received a call after one of these nights from Patrick's friend Eddie to let me know that Patrick was being detained out at the Riverhead, Long Island jail after being picked up the night before for a felony DUI charge. His car had been impounded, his driver's license taken away and his cell phone confiscated by police. I told his friend in no uncertain terms, "I'm not going to get him out. Let him rot there. It'll do him some good."

I had clearly had it. Eddie let out a burst of nervous laughter and said, "Yeah, he told me you'd probably say something like that." I replied, "Good. So we all understand each other." I was certainly not the passive and enabling woman. Yet, I was still unsure of exactly what the hell was going on.

You see, although these things would happen two or three times a year, the rest of the time I was living with a loving, hands-on-dad and caring partner. I had trouble finally piecing the puzzle together and learning through speaking with some experts, that not all alcoholics drink themselves into a stupor every day. Not all alcoholics are violent and erratic in their moods. Not all alcoholics are neglectful of daily responsibilities. Some are functioning alcoholics who are adept at hiding their disease except for occasional occurrences. When they do slip, they can completely go off the rails, leaving everyone scratching their heads in utter disappointment and confusion. That was my situation, for the better part of six years.

But this night in January of 2010 was different. The next day I was set to head into Manhattan to conduct what would be my first on-camera interview. The interview subject was Attorney Gloria Allred and the subject matter to be covered required me to be present and knowledgeable in my chair. Being professional has always been extremely important to me. Timeliness, preparation… these things are non-negotiable as far as I am concerned. I am actually a bit notorious for always being early to any appointment or meeting. I value other people's time and I value my own time and my reputation.

Patrick came home at 6:30 AM the morning of my interview with Gloria and he made a beeline into our son's room where he began snuggling with him on the shag rug in the nursery. We said little to each other but I was just... sad. On little sleep and a sorrowful feeling about where my relationship stood, I walked into our son's nursery to find my son cooing and giggling as his father played with him and tickled him on the floor. I turned and left, getting into a waiting limousine and heading into the city, notes in hand, to go to work. "How could he have done this to me on such an important day?" I thought, on the car ride in. At that moment I quietly contemplated a separation and it laid heavy on my heart as I made small talk with my driver.

I arrived at the hotel in midtown, midmorning. My makeup artist, Filis Forman, and I headed up to the hotel room that Gloria's colleague had agreed to let us film the interview in. I can't remember why, but Gloria's own room was unsuitable for the shoot. At Gloria's request, I sent Filis to her room to do her makeup while my cameraman Paul Brozen set up the camera and lights. I was now in full work mode, joking and laughing, sitting at my mark so the lights could be set, and I put my personal troubles on the backburner.

The room was tight and the shoot was a little awkward because you could see a bed in the shot. Beyond that, it was your standard two chair interview set up, and instead of sitting directly across from each other we would be rather close and caddie cornered for a tighter shot.

When Gloria and Filis emerged we were nearly ready to roll. I ran over to Gloria, gave her a hug and said, "You look beautiful!" I then turned to Filis and told her she did a fantastic job glamming Gloria up for the interview. The makeup was impeccable and Gloria was wearing her signature red suit. Filis whispered in my ear, "Look. She's in all red." I was kind of slow on the uptake and said, "Ok, yeah. Her suit is pretty." Filis shot me that "duh" look and whispered again, "No. Don't you get it? All.Red. *Allred*. Get it?!" Got it.

Gloria and I sat in our seats, got mic'd up and she said to me, "You look very pretty." We were on a tight budget so I had to do my own makeup and I commissioned Filis to just do Gloria's makeup. I thought I did a decent job, but it was by no means professional camera-ready makeup. Filis took some mercy on me and touched up my powder and blush a bit.

I will admit that at the time of this interview I felt that some of Gloria's positions leaned a bit towards the extreme and I can remember telling myself to take her with a grain of salt. I look back on that now and feel I was wrong. That point was really hit home for me when I recently watched the film, *Suffragette*. I witnessed in this film an unvarnished account of what these suffragettes endured in their courageous and self-sacrificing fight to gain women the right to vote. It's very easy to accuse those on the front lines of being angry, bitter, or overzealous and demagogues from our position of privilege. What I have come to realize is, I can afford to be nonchalant and to not give feminism and equal rights for women a second thought because others have and continue to fight the fight on my behalf. I can take my vote in our 2016 presidential election for granted. I can take for granted that I make a nice living and am taken seriously in my chosen profession. I can take for granted that I can own property, fight for my legal rights if need be and enjoy an overall good quality of life. Other women in the past sacrificed their freedom, their families, their jobs, their safety and their reputations so that I don't have to. Don't get it twisted. Whether you are of a minority race, a formerly persecuted religion, a member of the LGBTQ community, a woman, or simply an American enjoying your freedom, we all have blood on our hands. We are all the beneficiaries of other people's fight.

Here is an excerpt from my interview with Gloria that sheds some light on the dynamics of celebrity legal scandals:

Allison Kugel: Do you believe that someone who is wealthy and powerful can be victimized by someone who is not?

Gloria Allred: Yes. We have represented some celebrities, but generally we are representing non-celebrities against celebrities. Celebrities often will say that they are being victimized by the individuals who are suing them, and they come up with the standard, boring and unimaginative script-line that there is some kind of economic motive or criminal act that is being perpetrated on them

Allison Kugel: You don't sound convinced.

Gloria Allred: It's often not the case. Often they have hurt the non-celebrity and they have hurt them in a variety of ways. They are just rationalizing or engaging in spin to protect their own celebrity image rather than admitting, and taking responsibility for the wrong that they have inflicted on one of their employees, or someone with whom they've had an intimate relationship, or someone else in their life. So rather than acknowledging their personal responsibility and compensating the person whom they have harmed they will rationalize and try to make themselves the victim.

It's probably not something they are going to be able to defend in a court of law. But for the purposes of the court of public opinion they and their entourage will put that out in the public airwaves to try to sustain and maintain their own reputation.

Allison Kugel: Do you think that power and celebrity corrupt one's character?

Gloria Allred: I'm really not dealing with their character. I'm dealing with their PR image that they're trying to spin to their advantage. I understand why they do that, but sometimes that's going to bite them in the neck later on because they are unable to defend their actions in a court of law. They often have a bunch of "yes" people around them who are willing to do whatever the celebrity wants. Often, in the end, those same people end up getting fired, and sometimes those same people come to me to represent them against the celebrity . There have been many such cases. I know where all of the skeletons are buried in Southern California.

Allison Kugel: Why have you chosen to try certain cases in the court of public opinion?

Gloria Allred: We don't try cases in the court of public opinion. We assert our clients' rights.

Allison Kugel: Wouldn't holding a press conference be trying a case in the court of public opinion?

Gloria Allred: We don't ordinarily just do a press conference. We are doing something in addition to a press conference. We are doing a lawsuit and asserting a claim in some manner.

Allison Kugel: That much I understand, but why in certain cases, in addition to trying a case in a court of law, also hold a press conference and put it out there in the media?

Gloria Allred: Filing a lawsuit is a public record open to anyone who wishes to view it. So if we are also doing a news conference in addition to the filing of a lawsuit, we are helping to put into context, and give a frame of reference to the lawsuit that is already on file and will be viewed by the public, and may be written about and discussed.

Allison Kugel: Is it a way of leveling the playing field for your client, and giving them the same home- court advantage as the celebrity, so that once the lawsuit becomes public it's a more balanced story?

Gloria Allred: I think providing a frame of reference does help to level the playing field.

Allison Kugel: I want to talk to you about the term "feminism." You wear it proudly; you call yourself a feminist. In recent decades it has gotten a bad name. Why do you think that is?

Gloria Allred: A feminist is a person who believes in legal, social, political and economic equality for women with men. To me, if a person is not a feminist, well the opposite of a person who believes in equality would be a bigot, would be a person who believes that woman should be subordinated and should be second class citizens. To me it's like, you're either pregnant or you're not pregnant. There is no in between. You're either a feminist who believes in equality, or you're not. Why is it being given a bad name? Probably because some people don't know what it is, so they jump to the wrong conclusions, or they're against the concept of women enjoying equal rights with men

AK: But you agree that there is a strange stigma attached to the term...

Gloria Allred: For some reason there is. Even though the public policy of our nation is for equal rights for women, there is a strong strain of patriarchy still existing among some people. Those people prefer to stigmatize those of us who wish to, and do, fight for equal rights for women. It's as simple as that. Male chauvinism is, according to the American Psychiatric Association, a certifiable mental illness. But the good news is that it can be cured.

AK: Is that a joke or is that actually true?

Gloria Allred: It's absolutely true. Male chauvinism is dangerous to a woman's health. Most people would say that if people think that African Americans should enjoy a secondary citizenship status, that obviously that would be wrong! And it would not be a laughing matter. And yet, when [male] chauvinists somehow think that women should be subordinated and not enjoy equal rights, some people say, "Oh, that's funny . Could that really be?" Well, it's not funny. It's actually dangerous to a woman's health.

Left to right: Members of Anne Frank's family. Sister
Margot Frank, father Otto Frank and first cousin
Bernard "Buddy" Elias.
Courtesy of ANNE FRANK-FONDS, Basel,
Switzerland.

CHAPTER THIRTEEN

"Religion has always separated humanity, never united it."
– told to me by Bernard "Buddy" Elias, first cousin of Anne Frank

For every interview I have ever conducted there is a chain of events that took place from start to finish; from inception of an idea through the finished product of the article. Name a person I've interviewed and I can tell you exactly how I found their press representative and what went into booking the interview. That has been the case with all but one. I could not tell you how I came to know about Anne Frank's first cousin and last living direct relative, Mr. Bernard "Buddy" Elias. The details of how we got in touch are fuzzy, almost as if they didn't happen at all. Yet somehow I found myself embarking on one of the most fulfilling and historically relevant interviews of my journalism career. Looking back at this beautiful experience, I am more than sure that our meeting and collaboration was no accident, but divinely orchestrated with the help of my late grandfather, Papa Morty *(Morton Kugel)*.

I had recently said goodbye to my beloved grandfather, whom we called Papa, just several months prior to meeting Mr. Elias. Although I knew in my heart that my grandfather and I would meet again someday, the physical loss had been weighing on me heavily. My Papa, Morton Kugel, was born Martin Kugel on June 2, 1922 in New Haven, Connecticut, to poor Jewish eastern European immigrants who eventually moved my grandfather and his two older sisters to Brownsville, Brooklyn. My Papa's father Benjamin, was a laborer, a presser in the garment district of New York. He stood in a dank steamy room all day, manually pressing clothes for a living. They were so poor that my Papa slept on a cot in the family's tiny galley kitchen. As the story goes, one late night or early morning *(I can't remember which)* his two older sisters were boiling some water on the stove while my Papa was sleeping on his makeshift bed, when they accidentally spilled the pot of boiling water all over him. In the winter, my grandfather would go out to the railroad yard and steal coal to help the family heat their small cold water flat apartment. Other times, he shined shoes on the streets of Brooklyn to make some extra money to contribute to his father's meager income. One day my Papa was bent over shining shoes when he looked up in surprise to see that his father, my great grandfather Ben, was standing above him with a look of disgust on his face. He knocked over my Papa's shoeshine kit with a backhanded swipe and angrily yelled, "No son of mine is gonna shine shoes. GET UP!" I think he was angry at himself for not being able to provide better for his family.

My Papa managed to go to college and start a career as a professional musician in a band, but was then drafted into the army in short order to fight the Nazis in Europe during World War II. The guy had never even been out of his birth place of New Haven, Connecticut or Brooklyn, New York. But like countless other young boys, he found himself on the front lines of the United States Army's first infantry division with a rifle strapped to his back. He wasn't in an army kitchen or office shifting around papers; he was on the front lines fighting for his life and for the lives of countless others, both here and abroad. After getting hit with exploding pieces of shrapnel, getting shot in his left arm and being stuck in a foxhole for six months *(when we'd complain about anything he'd say, "Try being stuck in the same underwear for six months").* He was a stellar and fearless soldier and eventually eligible for promotion from the rank of Private. Thanks to the hot blooded Kugel temper, he would never get that much-deserved promotion.

My Papa was placed in charge of guarding some German Nazi POWs on the American base camp, and felt the need to straighten one prisoner out by beating the guy within an inch of his life with the butt of his rifle. What was it that set my Papa off? The German POW smugly said, "Hey Jew. We're having fun killing your people and raping your women."

My Papa might not have risen from the bottom rank of Private but he did play a pivotal role in liberating certain territories from Nazi control. He was awarded several medals posthumously, to boot, which my family and I collected during a ceremony a few years after his death. He came home to New York and promptly stole my grandmother *(Nanny)*, Thelma Ugelow, away from her current fiancé, marrying her before the other guy even knew what hit him. They had my dad Richard and my Uncle Barry, and my Papa went on to earn millions in the commercial lighting business. The bullet he took to his left arm in the army ensured that he would never achieve his original career aspirations of becoming a professional musician. Forgoing his young dreams of playing music for a living, he managed to create a beautiful life for his family and remained a strong and steadfast patriarch until his death in November 2007, at the age of 85, from lung and brain cancer.

Private Morton Kugel being honorably discharged from the army c.1945.

One early morning I turned on my computer to find an email that had a Swiss email handle. I opened up the email and there was a letter from a Mr. Bernard Elias. He introduced himself, explaining that he had gotten word through his organization, the Anne Frank-FONDS (the Swiss arm of the Anne Frank Foundation, which also has its origins in Amsterdam, Netherlands) that I was an American journalist who had been trying to reach him. Right away I knew who he was, as I had suddenly recalled reading an article about him where it was stated that he was Anne Frank's first cousin and only living direct relative. In that article he was referred to as Buddy, not Bernard. My mind put all of the pieces together and I began Googling like a madwoman. Bernard "Buddy" Elias was a notable Swiss actor who was also head of the Anne Frank-FONDS, which curates and manages the Frank family legacy as well as the famous Anne Frank house which still resides in Amsterdam, Netherlands, for public viewing. Buddy was handed the reins of the Frank family legacy by Anne Frank's father, the late Otto Frank. Otto was the only member of the Frank family to have survived the horrors of the Jewish concentration camps that were operated under Adolph Hitler's Nazi regime. Buddy Elias was Otto Frank's nephew and a trusted ally in helping Otto to preserve the writings and memory of his deceased daughter, Anne Frank. Otto Frank died in 1980 in Birsfelden, Switzerland. My Nanny and Papa had been extensive travelers in the last thirty years of their lives, visiting just about every country of consequence on the map. Shortly before my Papa's death, I interviewed him "on the record" with recording equipment in hand, and he made a great point of telling me that of all the places he and my grandmother had traveled, his favorite place on earth was Switzerland. I also noted through my research of Buddy Elias, that his birthday was June 2nd. Papa's birthday had also been June 2nd. I felt in my gut that these circumstances were no coincidence and that this amazing and historic opportunity had been given to me as a gift from my Papa. Papa Morty was extremely proud of my journalism career and my accomplishments. In fact, here is a small excerpt from the opening portion of my piece on Buddy Elias, published on May 6, 2008, which reiterates my above sentiments:

> I recently had the extreme privilege of speaking with Mr. Bernhard "Buddy" Elias who is Anne Frank's first cousin, as well as her last living direct relative. For this reason, I believe that Buddy Elias is a walking, breathing monument of human history. Unlike most interviews I have done, I have no memory of how I came to find Mr. Elias or what originally prompted me to seek him out. My memory only begins with our initial correspondence. In researching Buddy Elias's life I learned that his birthday is June 2nd, which is the same day as my beloved late Grandfather's birthday. I knew then that we were meant to do this interview together.

I remember feeling at the time that interviewing Mr. Elias and documenting his responses to my questions would be like witnessing and recording a piece of living history, and I was honored to be doing so. Being Swiss, Buddy was concerned about his somewhat fragmented and heavily accented English and that his memories of Anne were anecdotes that were special to him and his family, but nothing of the spectacular sort that would make me too excited. I assured him that any glimpse into Anne's brief life before World War II would be of extreme value to me and to countless others, just as her diary has been to the more than 25 million people across the globe who have read it *(Anne Frank: The Diary of a Young Girl, Doubleday 1952).*

You have to understand that for a Jewish child who was taught repeatedly about the Holocaust, about the life of Anne Frank, her diary, and stories about the Frank family's two years in hiding during the Nazi's dogged hunting, imprisoning and mass murdering of European Jews, to actually be granted a conversation with Anne's first cousin was awe inspiring and spectacular for me. I felt privileged beyond what I can express on these pages. At thirty-three years of age, it was like, "Mom, you taught me about the story and the book, but I'm actually friends with her 1st cousin! I am asking him all about Anne." Here I was, hearing stories from Buddy about the two of them playing dress up and how much Anne enjoyed impersonating their grandmother for laughs, right from the horse's mouth.

Of course, I did my very best to do this man's story and his precious memories justice. But when I received the below thank you letter from Mr. Elias my heart absolutely swelled.

Just days after my article was published, I received this email from Buddy:

> Thank you so much for the best interview that has ever been made about me. I have a feeling that I realy do not deserve that honour [sic].
>
> My wife also sends her thanks and best regards to you. Should you ever come to Switzeland while we are still alive, we would love to welcome you as our guest [sic].
>
> We wish you the best of luck, good health and success in your work.
>
> Yours sincerely
>
> Gerti and Buddy Elias
> First cousin of Anne Frank & Chairman of The Anne Frank-FONDS

I regret that I never did make that trip to Buddy's home in Switzerland to spend time with him and his wife. When I reached out just a year ago with news about this book, I received a somber reply from his assistant informing me that Buddy had just passed away and wishing me well with my book.

My heart felt heavy as I scrambled to Google News and saw that Buddy had just, only days before, passed away near his home in Switzerland. He will always remain an important piece in the tapestry of my life story.

CHAPTER FOURTEEN

"I find that when your spirit shines, everything looks more beautiful anyway." told to me by Elle Macpherson

I look back on my decade as a journalist with a big Cheshire cat grin, filled with gratitude for the people I met, the things I heard and learned, and the stories I shared with readers. It was a big, beautiful gift that I will always cherish. Many of the moments during these interviews were fun, funny, lighthearted and inspirational; encapsulated moments exempt from the laws of time and space where undefinable energy was exchanged. There were countless moments when being paid to do my job almost seemed immaterial, because I was so enriched by the experiences, themselves.

Discussing consumer advocacy and fighting the good fight up on Capitol Hill with Ralph Nader; Talking sexy lingerie with Elle Macpherson; Inside jokes from the set of *Glee* with Chris Colfer; Anecdotes about Frank Sinatra from his daughter Nancy; Relationship advice from *Mars/Venus* author

John Gray; Sharing stories with TLC's Rozonda "Chilli" Thomas about being single moms raising boys; Discussing the creation of Spider-Man with Stan Lee.

These experiences can never be taken away from me. They are intangibly part of my intellectual and emotional landscape. They are mine.

By 2014, between my contracted interviews with PR.com and freelancing through a group of syndicators I worked with, I had amassed a body of work that included more than two hundred interview profiles with newsmakers from film, television, music, books, sports, health and politics. I didn't know it at the time, but I was writing this book; I was writing my story.

Though college was an important part of my life, my truest education has come from life's electives. It's the people who've crossed my path, the people I've touched who have touched me. Telling other people's stories was one of the most therapeutic experiences of my life and for that I will always be grateful.

Here are some of my funniest, most inspirational, most enlightening, and most truthful moments surmised from a cross section of my interviews:

Talking Kids with TLC's Rozonda "Chilli" Thomas

Allison Kugel: TLC has always been about female empowerment for young women. You're the single mom of a teenage son. What has that journey been like for you, seeing life from the perspective of a teenage boy?

Rozonda "Chilli" Thomas: I've found that the only difference between boys and girls is the attention span. That's pretty much the difference to me, because at the end of the day and as a parent you have to equip yourself for whatever comes up, with a boy or a girl. There are some people that are better with boys or better with girls, but I think you should be the best you can be for whatever God gives you. I just put good morals and values in my son, and I've been doing that since he was a baby. That's all you can do, and you obviously have to pay attention to your child's personality. You see that very early on, and you have to shape the mold but you don't want to break it. You don't want to break their spirit. The teenage years are my least favorite, though my son is phenomenal. He does not get in trouble and he's not a bad kid. But the fact that they think they know so much. I tell him, "Tron, I'm telling you, I said the same thing to my mom!" They just have to go through certain things, become more mature and get that wisdom. You just want to shield them from all the bad but you can't do that.

AK: I know, I know. I'm going to go through that at some point as well. Right now I have a five year old boy.

Chilli: Oh wow! I love boys. I have nieces and I have a goddaughter and I am telling you, they are the most amazing kids. You can't say boys are better than girls or vice versa. It just depends upon their personality and how you as a parent shape and mold them, and who you have around them influencing them, both male and female. But just love that boy, and I need you to get him hooked on WWE. Even if you had a girl I would tell you the same thing. It's so good!

AK: Right now he's obsessed with superheroes. He runs around the house in his Iron Man, Spider-Man and Batman costumes all the time.

Chilli: *My* son at five, Oh My God, he loved Ninjas. And sometimes he would want to sleep in his Ninja outfit, and I'd be like, "Tron!"

AK: Yup!

Chilli: Or I'd say, "Ok, let's take a bath," and he'd put the mask on and he didn't want to move his face a certain kind of way because he was afraid that it might move the mask. It was hilarious.

AK: I know. They stay in character. It's crazy (laughs).

Chilli: It's awesome. Kids are the most amazing gift ever.

Talking Brain Surgeon Music Playlists with CNN's Dr. Sanjay Gupta

Allison Kugel: Something I found interesting from reading your book that I never knew is that surgeons have playlists of music that they like to listen to at the beginning, the middle and at the end of performing an operation.

Dr. Sanjay Gupta: Exactly. I do, and I think different surgeons have various strategies on how they handle it, but I like music and I'm always trying to mix it up. There was a time when I was always the youngest guy in the room. What's funny now is as I've gotten older, I'm forty-two, I'm turning into one of the older guys. But music is the one great common denominator. I can keep up with all the latest music when I'm operating, and I'm surrounded by young guys in their mid-to-late twenties and early thirties who are always swapping playlists. It's kind of fun.

AK: Can you take me through the typical playlist you listen to when you're performing brain surgery?

Dr. Sanjay Gupta: Here we go. This is literally from the last operation I did on Monday: Finger Eleven by Paralyzer; Weezer; Just Breathe by Eddie Vedder; You Are A Tourist by Death Cab for Cutie; Fidelity by Regina Spektor; The Only Living Boy In New York by Paul Simon; Hold On Hope by Guided By Voices; Painkiller by Turin Brakes; Fix You by Coldplay; and I got Moving Along by All American Rejects. And then I actually got back to Paralyzer which means the operation took almost two hours . I can tell how long my operation takes if I hear the same song again.

Talking Fan Mail with Glee Star Chris Colfer

Allison Kugel: I would think that young people out there who are gay would take comfort in watching your character on the show. It gives them a reflection of themselves to look to, which is something we really didn't have on television, even a decade ago. Do you get fan mail from young people telling you that?

Chris Colfer: Every day; usually in the hundreds. Either fan mail through the actual mail or on Facebook, on Twitter and on MySpace. People write to me every day telling me how glad they are that there is a character like Kurt, and how much they look up to him. It's very rewarding.

AK: They feel like they can relate.

Chris Colfer: Yes, and I almost feel like I did that on purpose. When I was growing up the only gay characters that were present in the media were loud and flamboyant and obnoxious, and sometimes annoying. I really didn't want to play Kurt that way, and I really didn't know anyone like that growing up. I did know tons of gay people, but they were always, especially in a conservative town where I grew up, they were always very shy and internal and had to hold their emotions in[side] because they weren't really allowed to express it. That's kind of how I wanted to play Kurt, kind of different from what has been seen. I think that maybe that's what people have been picking up on and have been happy to see.

AK: I feel like I am definitely showing my age, because I'm asking about fan mail and you're like, "No, people contact me on Facebook and Twitter."

Chris Colfer: That was a complete surprise for me. Not to say I was expecting fan mail, that's pretty vain, but I was expecting it to all come through the mail, like what you said. But I guess everything is digital now. Who actually writes a letter? Who pays forty-four cents to send a letter? *(Laughs)*.

AK: When I was a kid, if you were a fan of someone you mailed them a letter and they sent you an autographed headshot.

Chris Colfer: And now you can just copy and paste one.

AK: Do you find it hard to get through a scene with Jane Lynch without losing your focus and without laughing?

Chris Colfer: *(Laughs)*. Yes, absolutely! It's probably the hardest thing any of us have to do. She is so funny, and she will adlib and go off the script. Even things she says to you in between scenes are hysterical. She's a comedic genius and it's so hard. Sometimes you have to think about something really, really horrible like a tragedy of some kind just to get through it, because she's just that good.

Childbirth and Push Presents with
Melissa Rivers

Melissa Rivers: When you're having a baby, you need drugs to be able to take that in.

Allison Kugel: I did it with no drugs.

Melissa Rivers: Are you *high*?! Why?

AK: My mother had natural childbirth and she convinced me I could do it.

Melissa Rivers: My mom told me that too, but you know that's a great big giant lie. My mom was like, "I didn't have anything! They gave me one shot of painkiller and that was it." You know what that shot was? I finally figured it out. They gave them Demerol IV. No wonder they didn't feel anything !

AK: I don't like drugs. They told me I could take Demerol or narcotic painkiller, or the Epidural or Spinal Block. I don't like narcotic drugs, and no one was sticking a needle into my spine, so I was out of options.

Melissa Rivers: I was all about the Epidural. I had Cooper when Cindy Crawford did the Gurmukh Yoga and everyone was doing the home birth, and my OB gave me a great piece of advice. She said, "In all the years that I've delivered babies I have never seen any [baby] turn to the mother after natural childbirth and say 'thank you.'"

AK: If I have another one I'll go for the Epidural. Natural childbirth once in a lifetime is enough.

Melissa Rivers: I hope you got a "push" gift. If not, you're owed a big one. Whatever he was going to spend, double it! I tell all my guy friends, "Don't even think about showing up at the hospital without a push gift." hospital without a push gift. And you went natural. Every now and then walk around and wince, and when he asks what's wrong with you just say, "Oh nothing, just residual pain."

AK: (Laughs).

Talking with Host of PBS's Finding Your Roots, Dr. Henry Louis Gates, Jr.

Allison Kugel: Was there an example in particular that really surprised the guest?

Henry Louis Gates, Jr: Stephen Colbert was one of my favorite guests. He was this super ultra-Irishman, but it turns out that one important line that came to America very early was a Lutheran German, and it blew his mind. He couldn't believe it, and he loved it, he loved it! And this is very important what I am about to say; no African-American that we have ever tested is 100% black, none! The average African-American is about 20% white in their DNA. Amazing!

AK: That's a foregone conclusion, isn't it? Because of slavery?

Henry Louis Gates, Jr: Yeah, but when you look at dark black people, people didn't think that was the case. Chris Rock is 20% white. Don Cheadle is 19% white. That's an amazingly high percentage.

AK: Back in February, which is obviously Black History Month, I happened to see the mini-series *Roots* being offered on my television's On-Demand menu. I decided to watch all of it, since I had never seen it before, and it's a classic. Although I had obviously learned about slavery in textbooks, I never made the emotional connection until I saw it on the screen, and then I got it! And I really feel like that mini-series should be mandatory curriculum for anyone who resides in the United States.

Henry Louis Gates, Jr: Me too, and at the time it was. The whole country watched. You cannot imagine the phenomenon of *Roots* in 1977. Everybody watched it. Other than during a crisis when everybody is watching the president speak, none of us has ever been part of anything like that. The whole country watched the mini-series for a week. Everybody was talking about it, all day long. It was phenomenal.

AK: If you look at a situation like the Trayvon Martin case, we are clearly still carrying some of that baggage as a nation.

Henry Louis Gates, Jr: No question, we're carrying a lot of that baggage. My series, *Finding Your Roots*, shows that, one, we're all immigrants; and two, we are all cousins. Genetically, we are all cousins. That is of utmost importance. If I have a larger humanitarian hope for this series, you want to entertain people but I'm a professor and I want to teach people. The larger political point that the series makes is that either through forced sexuality or voluntarily, and we have examples of both...

AK: There was more interracial and inter-cultural procreation than we realize.

Henry Louis Gates, Jr: Branford Marsalis, he descends from a white German man who shows up in New Orleans in 1851 and lives with a black woman named Mertay Valentine. They had seven kids, they died two years apart, and they're buried together. He had no idea, but there it was. That was as close to a legitimate relationship as you can get.

AK: Because Mertay Valentine was a free black woman.

Henry Louis Gates, Jr: On the other hand, [Brown University] President Ruth Simmons descends from the master who owned her ancestor. Can you have a relationship of equality with someone you own? Black people debate that all the time. But the point is, we are a mixed people.

DJ Pauly D on Britney Spears

Allison Kugel: This is a really important question: A few years ago, say back in 2008, did you ever think you would have Britney Spears's thighs wrapped around your head?

DJ Pauly D (Paul DelVecchio): *(Laughs).* Never in a million, million, million years! I never thought Britney Spears would even know I existed, let alone to give me a lap dance on stage in front of twenty-thousand people.

AK: How'd Britney wind up giving you a lap dance?

DJ Pauly D (Paul DelVecchio): I've been on the Britney tour. When I DJ with her on her tour, I do my act, then Nicki Minaj would go on, and then Britney would go on. I always stay for the second two acts because I'm a fan of both of them. So Britney called me on stage and the dancers brought me up, and she sat me down and gave me that lap dance . I did not expect that at all.

AK: What was going through your mind?

DJ Pauly D (Paul DelVecchio): I couldn't stop smiling and I was like, "Is this even real?" I didn't even know what went on. When it was done, I was like, "What just happened?!" Who in their lifetime can say they got a lap dance from Britney Spears?

The Invention of Spider-Man with Stan Lee

Allison Kugel: Could you ever have imagined that Spider-Man 1 and Spider-Man 2 would go on to be two of the biggest box office openers of all time? (As of the date of this article, Spider-Man 1, biggest opening weekend; Spider-Man 2, biggest opening Wednesday.)

Stan Lee: I imagined it when the movies were being made, because I realized how well they were being made. But in the early days, when we were doing the books, I never thought that would become the world wide icon that he is. I just hoped the books would sell and I'd keep my job.

AK: You certainly kept your job! Why are these stories that you wrote all coming to the screen now? Fantastic Four, Spider-Man, X-Men, Daredevil, Hulk... everything has come to the screen in the last couple of years. Why now?

Stan Lee: One reason is that a new group took over [Marvel], and they were dedicated to doing these movies. In the past, the people running Marvel really weren't making any great effort to do motion pictures of the characters. The second reason is the fact that the technology had evolved to the point where the special effects could be done so magnificently now. *Spider-Man* couldn't have been done as well as it was, 10 years ago. They couldn't have had him swinging on the web the way he did, and so forth. And the reason that so many of the comic book superheroes are coming to the screen is simply because now they're able to do it, and they weren't able to before.

AK: You're right. I never thought of that. In the movie Hulk, the animation was so real, so detailed. They could not have done that probably even 7 or 8 years ago.

Stan Lee: Absolutely right. It all started, I think, When *Superman* first came out and the ad said: "You will believe a man can fly." You remember?

AK: Oh, when the first Superman came out? Oh gosh, I think I was really little. (Laughs) Sorry.

Stan Lee: Well I remember Noah's Ark. I keep forgetting.

AK: Laughs.

Stan Lee: That was the start of it. But even then, they couldn't have done what they do now with a movie like *Spider-Man* or *X-Men*, or *The Hulk*.

AK: And you co-wrote all three Spider-Man scripts. Is that correct?

Stan Lee: No. What happened was *Spider-Man 1* and *2*, the screenplays were taken… I'd say *Spider-Man 1*, about 95% of it was based on the stories I had written, and *Spider-Man 2*, about 90% was based on stories I had written. I don't actually write screenplays.

AK: For Spider-Man 3, did they make up their own original story?

Stan Lee: Well they're using characters from the books, but I think it's going to be… they're taking bits from a lot of different books. I haven't read the script myself, so I only know what I've heard.

AK: And have you been involved at all on set for any of these movies?

Stan Lee: I do my thing and they do their thing. The only time I go on the set is when I have a cameo to do in the picture. I go to the set and I do my little cameo and I meet all the people. It's a great way to spend the day. And then I go back to my own world.

AK: How did that tradition start, with you making a cameo appearance in every movie?

Stan Lee: I think it started with . No, with the
. It was in the first   movie. There was this
scene on the beach, and they had me selling
hotdogs in the background while something
went on. You only saw me on the screen for a
couple of seconds. But being the perfectionist
that I am, I kept saying to the director, Bryan
Singer, "What is my motivation? Should this
hot dog that I'm trying to sell have mustard
and sauerkraut?" ...

AK: ... "Is it kosher, or isn't it?" (Laughs)

Stan Lee: ... "Is it rare?"... I mean, I really care
about these things.

Tyrese & Film Director John Singleton Discuss Their Friendship

**Allison Kugel: What do you think John
Singleton sees in you, and why does he
want to keep making movies with you?**

Tyrese Gibson: John Singleton is my hero. *(At
this point Tyrese tells me he would prefer
that I ask John Singleton to explain to me
why he chooses to keep casting Tyrese in his
movies, and proceeds to get him on three-way
conference call).*

Tyrese Gibson *(to John Singleton)*: It's Tyrese. I'm doing an interview and she wants to know what does John Singleton keep seeing in you? What is it about you that makes John want to keep working with you? And I really couldn't answer it, so I figured I would call you up and see if you'd be interested in answering that question.

John Singleton: I don't know. He's like my little brother. I just can't get rid of him, that's all.

AK: Alright then, that's the answer I'm putting down (Laughs).

John Singleton: [Tyrese] is mad at me 'cause I missed his concert in L.A. He was like, "You don't care about nobody. We're old friends. How come you don't support me?" So I showed up at his studio at 12:30 in the morning and I went off on him.

Tyrese Gibson: *(Laughs)*.

John Singleton: And I said, "I got my own responsibilities as a man but I'm still your f**king friend, so shut the f*ck up."

Tyrese Gibson: *(Laughs)*.

John Singleton: And then we hung out till 4:30 in the morning.

Tyrese Gibson: Yeah. We got a love/hate relationship.

AK: Are you guys around the same age?

Tyrese Gibson : John, I'm 27. How old are you?

John Singleton: I'm 38. I'm 11 years older than him. The cool thing [is] we're both from the same environment. The things that we've seen at an early age, it's phenomenal that we're not destroyed as men. We're still rising. We're still shining. Even though we work in the entertainment industry, we don't have the airs of the kind of people... a lot of people in this business, they re-invent themselves to a degree that they don't know who they are anymore. That's what he and I share. We're sophisticated but we're still ghetto.

AK: (to John Singleton): Why'd you stalk Tyrese into doing your film, Baby Boy? Why'd you come banging on his door?

John Singleton: He told you that?! *(We all laugh).*

John Singleton: I wanted him to be in [the movie] *Shaft*. He read for [the movie] *Baby Boy* two and a half years before we even did it, and then he just read a little bit of it, like a few lines. I said, "Ok. I want you to be in *Shaft*, in the beginning of it, in the first scene. And he was doing the MTV thing. He was like, "No man." And then he wouldn't accept my calls. You remember that?

Tyrese Gibson: Yeah, I remember.

John Singleton: He wouldn't accept my calls because he was, like, so scared. He was too nervous to try to do it; to act. So then *Shaft* comes out, and it's all over the billboards and television and everything. Then he said, "I'm sorry." He gave me a long-ass, 10-minute message on my cell. "I'm so sorry man. I see all the advertising. I see your vision. You still want me to do this movie thing? I'm down with it." So then I had him come back and I went over his house and gave him the script for *Baby Boy*. He was living in a little condo in Gardena.

Tyrese Gibson: My house wasn't little, by the way. It was not a condo.

AK: What's wrong with a condo?

Tyrese Gibson: It was not a condo! It was a four bedroom, brand new house, with a two car garage. He trippin'.

AK: (Laughs).

Tyrese Gibson: Don't downsize me, God damn it, to a condo!

John Singleton: Anyway, I went over there and gave him the script and was like, "Read the script." He said, "No, no. Just tell me about it." He was telling me to read the damn script to him and I was getting pissed off! I was like, "Take this f**king script and read this script!" *(We all laugh.)*

AK: (to Tyrese): You wanted it read to you word for word?

Tyrese Gibson: He was over there trying to sell me on the script and I was still in my little music mode. I wasn't really interested in acting. So he got frustrated and said, "M*ther f*cker, read the script!" He bullied me. So I read the script and we ended up doing the movie 'cause I loved it. So that's the story behind *Baby Boy*. That's how I started acting.

John Singleton: That's that public Watts school education. That's a true story.

Tyrese Gibson: You're the only person on earth other than Jesus Christ who saw something in me that I didn't see in myself. Because I've never been more rebellious towards such a big opportunity. I've never given anybody so huge, as far as a director, producer, writer... so much friction against not doing something that he wants me to do. And then once I did it, it ended up being the biggest thing I've ever done in my life. Imagine being on a movie set, when everything you hear about Hollywood is all fake. They complement you and they don't really mean it. It's a bunch of ego strokers. They don't really mean what they say on most movie sets. So the whole time I'm on the set of *Baby Boy*, he's like, "Oh, man! That was incredible!" John Singleton [was] getting all fired up and excited over certain scenes I was doing. The whole time I was appreciating it, but I didn't believe that he was really that excited.

AK: You thought it was just B.S.

Tyrese Gibson: I thought it was that Hollywood shit that I always heard about. Once the movie came out and people were running up to me telling me what they thought, that's when it started all hitting home for me. So then I recognized that maybe there is something really there that I didn't realize. For John Singleton to see that in me and I didn't see it in myself… that's why I dedicate so much of my success and where I am as an actor to him. That's a part of the reason we keep working together, too. I know that John Singleton is never going to move on and do another scene until I am at my best. He knows when I'm at my best. So I think we have a great chemistry, and I think we are one film away from Denzel Washington and Spike Lee, with the amount of films that they did. That's why we're trying to figure out which next film we're going to do to change the world together.

AK: (to John Singleton): See, you're responsible for inspiring and encouraging another person. If it wasn't for you, he never would have known that he had this talent.

John Singleton: He knew he had the talent...

AK: Well, he didn't have the confidence. Thank you for that.

Michelle Rodriguez on Hollywood & Director James Cameron

Allison Kugel: Could you ever play a character that's not a tomboy?

Michelle Rodriguez: Definitely. As long as she doesn't have to rip her clothes off.

AK: You would never do nudity?

Michelle Rodriguez: It's not that I would never do nudity. It's just that the grand majority of the time that it's done it's the same old story... girl looking for guy; guy leaves girl; girl is broken hearted and you can't wait for them to get back together. If I have to hear that story one more time I'll want to shoot myself.

AK: So no romantic comedies for you.

Michelle Rodriguez: The day that somebody approaches me with something interesting then I'll definitely work hard to try to be a part of it.

AK: How did you win your role in *Avatar*?

Michelle Rodriguez: According to Jim [Cameron], a while back he had taken a trip on a chopper in some cold place. I don't know if it was Antarctica; it was one of his adventure trips. One of his adventure trips there was this female pilot who was flying this chopper. I guess she made an impression on him because at one point she did this crazy difficult maneuver off of this glacier, and he almost shat his pants. At that point he realized that this would be a great character to incorporate into *Avatar* and then he thought of me. He had seen some of my work in *Girlfight* and in Lost, and I was surprised. I was like, "What? Are you kidding me?! I love your work!"

AK: What happened between *Lost* and *Avatar*? For a while, your reputation was less than stellar. So what happened in that time period?

Michelle Rodriguez: Nothing really happened in that time period. At the end of the day Hollywood is filled with a bunch of followers. There aren't many leaders in Hollywood. So if you get a bad reputation, you're going to go down and you're gonna do some time without working. And that's exactly what happened. After *Lost* … I got lost! People thought, "She's like all those little girls who go around partying all the time."

AK: Was that a fair assessment?

Michelle Rodriguez: Not at all. Are you kidding me?? I went to jail for a glass and a half of wine… on a holiday. Relax people. That was three years ago. I wasn't running around at three o'clock in the morning coming out of a party or stumbling out of a bar. It's not like that; they put me in the wrong category. It wasn't until James Cameron came out and said, "I want you to be a part of this project." I said, "You do acknowledge that Hollywood thinks I'm crazy." And he's like, "You're not crazy." So next thing you know they're calling me up for *Fast & Furious (The Fast And The Furious film franchise)* and now Neal Moritz is working with me again, and boom! I'm back in the saddle.

My Panty Party with Elle Macpherson

Allison Kugel: Were you that much of a tomboy?

Elle Macpherson: No, I wasn't really a tomboy. I loved sports and I still do, so I dressed practically, for my beach lifestyle. Today I like to snow ski, water ski, play tennis, hike, ride horses, but I don't think that makes me a tomboy. When it came to modeling swimwear or beachwear I was fine, and when it came to lingerie I just knew exactly what to do. I have a body where the proportions work really well for that kind of clothing. I would just put my hair all over my face and somehow it worked.

AK: So when they put you in high fashion you didn't know what to do with yourself.

Elle Macpherson: Yeah, I didn't know what to do with myself *(laughs)*. I would start laughing. I felt like those girls who dress up in their mother's clothes!

AK: Do you always wear your lingerie under your clothes?

Elle Macpherson: Always, and always matching. If I get dressed and then I decide to change my shirt and I have to change my bra because of the color, I would have to take off my pants and change my knickers as well. I can't be miss-matched. It's like wearing odd socks! I have a younger sister who makes fun of me and says, "It is so old-fashioned to wear matchy-matchy," and I say, "I don't care. I'm nearly fifty. I'm going to keep wearing matchy-matchy…"

AK: (Laughs).

Elle Macpherson: She wears different bottoms and different tops, and she says that's much cooler.

AK: Personally, I don't usually wear underwear, because I find you either get a panty line, or with a thong you find yourself with a permanent wedgy for the day. How do you make the underwear work underneath your clothes?

Elle Macpherson: I'll have to give you some of my lingerie. They're very comfortable, and you might just change your mind and say, "Actually, I really like wearing these." The lingerie that we design is French style with an American fit. It's comfortable, beautiful and sexy, and no VPL *(visible panty line)*.

Getting a Special Gift from Tupac Shakur's Mother, Afeni Shakur

In early 2005, after Oscar nominations were announced, I found out the documentary film *Tupac: Resurrection* about the life of the late rapper Tupac Shakur, had been nominated in the category of Best Documentary Feature Length Film. The team from Amaru Entertainment and MTV Films would be attending the ceremony. That same month I was scheduled to interview attorney, Dina LaPolt, who was in charge of Tupac

Shakur's estate, along with his mother Afeni Shakur. After Tupac's 1996 death, Dina and Afeni worked together tirelessly to untangle more than $10 million in royalties and other assets owed to Tupac that he never lived to receive. According to Dina. Once monies and ownership of her son's name and estate were recovered, Afeni had the resources to establish The Tupac Amaru Shakur Foundation and the Tupac Amaru Shakur Center for the Performing Arts to continue her son's legacy.

In February of 2005, I interviewed *Tupac: Resurrection* co-producer Dina LaPolt about Amaru Entertainment's Oscar nomination for the film and the work that was involved in recovering and establishing Tupac's estate. Here is some of that interview.

Allison Kugel: You and your law firm, LaPolt Law, represent Tupac Shakur's entire estate?

Dina LaPolt: Yes. Tupac's mother, Afeni Shakur, and her entertainment companies, which fall under the umbrella of Amaru Entertainment, Inc. Amaru [was] Tupac's middle name. I do all the entertainment transactional work; the record company, all the films, the books, the merchandising, the clothing line, all of that. We have a foundation lawyer down in Atlanta, and I work very closely with her.

AK: Afeni hired you after the death of her son?

Dina LaPolt: I met her in August 1998 when I was at my old firm, and she and I hit it off right away. I was just a little bitty associate at my old firm, and it was my boss who she had hired through referral. I can tell you that I basically grew up practicing law with Afeni Shakur.

AK: You're responsible for freeing up millions of dollars in frozen assets and unpaid royalties to Tupac. Where were these assets and how did you untangle them?

Dina LaPolt: When Tupac died, he never had a music lawyer. When you are a recording artist every royalty payment that goes to producers and other third party royalty participants , comes out of the artist's royalty. And if they write music with the artist, then the artist has to do agreements with them, like song split agreements. So these people share in the publishing money. When Tupac died, nothing was papered on his behalf. Under the terms of his recording agreement, they were still allowed to release all his albums notwithstanding the fact that none of the paperwork was done. They just didn't pay him. They froze all the royalty streams and kept their profits. When I got involved, there was literally over $13 million dollars in frozen royalty payments that belonged to Tupac, to his producers, to all his co-writers... it was just awful. Me, in connection with another lawyer, Donald David, who was very influential in getting this untangled as well, and the lawyer for our publishing company, Robert Allen, for two and a half years of our lives we just went song by song and worked out all the copyright splits.

AK: Did any of that money have to go to Suge Knight?

Dina LaPolt: No. By the time I got involved, Donald David had already litigated Death Row [Records] and Suge Knight, and got all the intellectual properties reverted to Afeni Shakur. When I got involved, the estate was in a very litigious time. And I was the person who was brought in to help make it into a business. [Suge Knight] has two record albums that he still owns that are now distributed by Koch Records. He gets royalties on those, and he also gets royalties on some of the albums that we have on Interscope.

AK: The nine albums that were released after Tupac's death, where did all of the material come from?

Dina LaPolt: Tupac, when he died, left behind 154 unreleased master recordings. He told everyone he was gonna die. I mean if you've seen the film, [you] see the end when he says, "I don't have time here!" He goes, "I don't have time to lay the hook! You do that after I leave!"

AK: Why did he think he was going to die young?

Dina LaPolt: He just did. Even in the movie, you heard him say, "When I'm gone, you're gonna have all this material to be released." And as he's talking, they showcased each album we've released over the years. After being around Afeni Shakur all these years, I can tell you that it was probably a prophecy. Because she [also] knows things. She'll say to me, "You better put this in the contract, because in this many years this is gonna happen."

AK: What are the mechanics of working with an artist, posthumously?

Dina LaPolt: Working with a deceased artist is a lot harder, especially at the record company level. When Tupac's albums come out, Tupac is not there to yell at somebody when his video is not out when it's supposed to be. Tupac's not here to pick up the phone and say to the president of the record company, "Hello! What are you doing?! I want a list of all the radio stations that are playing my music." It was great this past album working with Eminem, because he was in Tupac's role. It was phenomenal. We love Eminem!

AK: Eminem and Afeni Shakur co-produced the Loyal to the Game album which was just released (2005)...

Dina LaPolt: Tupac is one of the biggest influences in Eminem's life and he'll tell you that within 5 minutes of meeting him.

AK: Then he and I have something in common.

Dina LaPolt: I was at a music conference in Boston and Afeni calls me and goes, "Dina, Oh My God! I got the cutest letter from Eminem!" He personally wrote to her and said, "Dear Afeni. I would like to produce the entire album. I am such a huge fan of your son." It was the sweetest letter. Afeni said, "I'm faxing the letter to your office for the files." A couple hours later I call my office to check in and my assistant Heidi says, "We got some random fax from a guy named Marshall. He says he wants to produce the next Tupac album. I put it in your unsolicited pile." I said, "Heidi, that's Eminem!!"

When this article posted to the website PR.com in its entirety, I got an email from Dina stating that Afeni loved the article so much that she was posting it on Tupac Shakur's official website. Afeni also shipped me a package filled to the brim with memorabilia from her son's amazing career: CDs, books, photographs… I was overjoyed and so pleased that my article made Afeni Shakur happy. I teared up earlier this year when I found out about her passing, but I know she is with her son in heaven.

You might have noticed from several of my interview excerpts and personal stories that when I am not swapping deep insights with people, my sense of humor is important to me and it's an integral part of my personality. I love to laugh at myself and I love to laugh with others. One of the things on my bucket list is to be roasted by my friends and family. In my mind, a roast is the highest of complements. It means these are people who are true blue in your life and vice versa. They know you so well that they can systematically dismantle you and get it 100% right, and at the same time they love you. In fact when my cousin Brandon and I get together, nothing is sacred; nothing's off limits. Everything is fair game to be made fun of and I love that about him. He gets it.

These days I know myself more than I ever have. I've taken inventory because I've had to. I own my strengths and I accept my weaknesses. I know when I am kicking ass and I admit to myself when it's time for a spiritual or emotional tune up. I am not averse to seeking out talk therapy, taking the time to meditate and breathe, revisiting my gratitude journal and even reviewing passages from the bible for extra guidance. And I couldn't, in good conscience, leave out the fact that I do take a small amount of medication.

I don't want you to think that I waved a magic wand and no longer ever experience anxiety. That would be a lie. However, I have hit bottom as you've read in previous chapters, and being armed with more insight and wisdom than ever before, I have the tools to bounce and come back better than ever. I am strong and confident in the notion that I will never unpack and live in that place again.

I know that our weaknesses can often make us tempted to run and hide out of shame and fear of what others may think of us, but I refuse to ever run or hide and I encourage you not to either. Whether you live with anxiety and panic, addiction, an eating disorder, mental illness, physical illness or what have you, face the world's perceptions head on and be a beacon of light for someone else who is walking your path a few steps behind you.

I am always open about what I have been through and what it's taken to get to where I am. In fact, I can remember one night during those bleakest of days in the summer of 2012. During one of my several trips to the ER, I sat up on the hospital cot and said a prayer to God. I prayed to God that if He would get me well again I would be vocal about anxiety and panic disorder and offer help to anyone who crossed my path who was going through the same thing. And I have kept that promise. I am always willing to lend an ear and share the tools I have accrued with someone in need. And I always will.

I also learned that I don't need much accompanying me in my earthly travels. I need the people I love and hold dear; I need my mementos – the material items

I have received in love like family jewelry heirlooms, photographs, books and such; and I need my Nutri-Bullet blender. I could literally wonder this earthly plane with a tote bag or backpack filled with these few items, side by side with those I love and God up above. I take great comfort in looking into another's eyes and hearing their story. It's my life's work, after all.

These days life is good, but I no longer need it to be perfect. At forty, I threw caution to the wind and took up horseback riding, a hobby where you feel free and so alive, but not completely in control. You've got 1,000 lbs. of spirited horse between your legs and you've got to form a synergy and spiritual connection with that horse, and hope to remain in sync during each ride.

I recently took my son boogie boarding in the ocean and we had a blast. During that afternoon as we were riding the waves in Fort Lauderdale, Florida, I thought, "Oh my God! Why have I never done this before?? It's so much fun! Where have I been all these years that it has taken me to the age of forty-one to go boogie boarding?" Meanwhile, my son was enjoying it at the age of seven. I envied him.

Perhaps it's because something as uncontrollable as ocean waves wouldn't have appealed to me before; too many variables. Too much up and down. But I liked it. No, I loved it! I'm learning to ride the waves without fear.

My life has changed a lot since hanging up my journalism hat in 2014. I still write a good amount as a blog contributor for The Huffington Post, Entrepreneur.com and for many of my public relations clients at my company, Full Scale Media. In fact, I am proud to share that I managed to get the eulogy I spoke at my Nanny's 2014 funeral published on the Huffington Post; my first article for them. It was a bit of an off-the-wall idea to pitch it to them, but I submitted it and they published it. I beamed with pride as I shared the published eulogy with friends and family who knew and loved my dad's mother, my Nanny.

And would you believe it? I'm now in the tech world and it's a family affair. My brother Jared and I invented the Upitch App; the first mobile app that matches public relations pitches with targeted journalists. From entertainment journalist to techie. Suffice to say, I no longer laugh or roll my eyes when someone makes an outside-the-box prediction for what they think I might be up to in 5 years. Anything is possible. Okay, confession time... I didn't even know what an app was until two years ago. Now I've invented one.

My son is now seven years old and one of the smartest, funniest and most caring human beings I have ever known; my creation. ☺

As I sit overlooking my backyard lake, I observe the ducks who reside on my property. Through their ease of existence and their innate ability to be one with nature, I grow reflective. I look back through these chapters you've just read with a smile and a laugh, as if it's my own inside joke.

As Frank Sinatra stated in his iconic anthem, *My Way*:

> "I've lived. I've laughed and cried. I've had my fill, my share of losing.
>
> And now, as tears subside, I find it all so amusing.
>
> To think, I did all that. And may I say, not in a shy way.
>
> Oh no. Oh no, not me. I did it my way.

Thanks for reading my mom's book. Love
Marcus! ☺

Acknowledgments

This project was a lifetime in the making, so I want to thank the people who made me. To Benjamin and Sophia Kugel and Sarah and Abraham Ugelow, my great grandparents; my story began with you.

To Morton and Thelma Kugel and Honore and David Rothenberg; you allowed the story to continue.

To Shelley and Richard Kugel, my parents; thank you for building me. To Jared Kugel and David Kugel, my brothers; thanks for growing up in the same house as me and for continuing to be two of my best friends. To my cousin, and brother from another mother, Brandon Reif; thank you for always bringing the laughter.

To Patrick Campbell; thank you for the gift of a lifetime. To Jason Manheim; thank you for the opportunity of a lifetime.

To Frankie the shih ztu and to Gem the horse; thank you for the unconditional love and for allowing me to learn to ride with you as my partner, respectively.

To Sheldon Wright; thank you for thinking I'm the greatest thing since sliced bread.

To my son, Marcus; thank you for choosing me to be your mom, teaching me about love, showing me the world through your eyes, and for simply being *you*. I love you.

To my entire posse in heaven, including my great grandparents, grandparents and some dear friends who have moved on to the next plane of existence…

who the hell has been sending me all those pennies?!

CPSIA information can be obtained
at www.ICGtesting.com
Printed in the USA
BVOW07s2057170717
489525BV00002B/10/P